ENVIRONMENTAL PIONEERS

PROFILES

Amazing Archaeologists and Their Finds
America's Most Influential First Ladies
America's Third-Party Presidential Candidates
Black Abolitionists and Freedom Fighters
Black Civil Rights Champions
Charismatic Cult Leaders
Courageous Crimefighters
Environmental Pioneers
Great Auto Makers and Their Cars
Great Justices of the Supreme Court
Hatemongers and Demagogues
Hoaxers and Hustlers
International Terrorists
Journalists Who Made History
Legendary Labor Leaders
Philanthropists and Their Legacies
Soviet Leaders from Lenin to Gorbachev
Top Entrepreneurs and Their Businesses
Top Lawyers and Their Famous Cases
Treacherous Traitors
Utopian Visionaries
Women Business Leaders
Women Chosen for Public Office
Women in Medicine
Women Inventors and Their Discoveries
Women of the U.S. Congress
Women Who Led Nations
Women Who Reformed Politics
The World's Greatest Explorers

ENVIRONMENTAL PIONEERS

Patricia Byrnes

The Oliver Press, Inc.
Minneapolis

The publisher wishes to thank **Shirley A. Briggs** and **David Brower** for their careful reviews of Chapters 6 and 7, respectively.

The Oliver Press, Inc.
Charlotte Square
5707 West 36th Street
Minneapolis, MN 55416-2510

Library of Congress Cataloging-in-Publication Data

Byrnes, Patricia
Environmental pioneers / Patricia Byrnes
p.   cm.—(Profiles)
Includes bibliographical references and index.
    Summary: Profiles people who have been influential in the environmental movement: John Muir, Jay Norwood "Ding" Darling, Rosalie Edge, Aldo Leopold, Olaus and Margaret Murie, Rachel Carson, David Brower, and Gaylord Nelson.
ISBN 1-881508-45-5 (library binding)
1. Environmentalists—United States—Biography—Juvenile literature. [1. Environmentalists.] I. Title. II. Series: Profiles (Minneapolis, Minn.)
GE55.B97   1998
363.7' 0092'2—dc21
[B]   97-30233
                                          CIP
                                          AC

ISBN 1-881508-45-5
Profiles XXVI
Printed in the United States of America
04 03 02 01 00 99 98   8 7 6 5 4 3 2 1

Contents

The native inhabitants of North America are sometimes referred to as the continent's original environmentalists because they used only the resources they needed to survive.

Introduction

*I*n 1642, Miantonomo, a chief of the Narragansett American Indian tribe, described his land after the arrival of the white settlers on the East Coast:

> Our fathers had plenty of deer and skins, our plains were full of deer, as also our woods, and of turkies [sic] and our coves full of fish and fowl. But these English having gotten our land, they with scythes cut down the grass, and with axes fell the trees; their cows and horses eat the grass and their hogs spoil our clam banks, and we shall all be starved.

Believing that the nation's natural resources were endless, European settlers from east to west repeated this destructive pattern of behavior again and again over the next 250 years. Hunters shot birds so that stylish ladies could adorn their hats with beautiful feathers. In 1886 alone, according to the American Ornithologist Union, hunters killed an estimated 5 million North American birds for fashion. The once abundant bison, often called buffalo, were slaughtered by the millions—sometimes only for their tongues, considered a delicacy of the day. From New England to the Great Lakes to the southern

The "sport" of shooting bison from trains contributed to the near extinction of these animals. In the early 1800s, an estimated 60 million bison roamed across most of the western United States and Canada. By the end of the century, only two small herds of a few hundred remained, one in Yellowstone National Park and the other in Canada.

Appalachian Mountains, settlers cut down the forests that had stood for millennia. One ancient saying claimed that before the Europeans arrived, a squirrel could travel tree-to-tree from the Atlantic Ocean to the Mississippi River without ever touching the ground. Moving west, ranchers let their cattle and sheep overgraze the lush grasses that once covered the plains and meadows, leaving behind only weeds and eroded soil.

The first phase of the modern environmental movement occurred in the last half of the nineteenth century. Those concerned with the natural world during this era were called *conservationists* because they concentrated on conserving, or saving, the nation's resources, such as rivers and forests and grasslands, from development. These conservationists often were naturalists or philosophers. A *naturalist* is someone who studies plants, animals, rocks, or anything else in the natural world. John Muir, the father of the American environmental movement, was a naturalist and writer whose words and wisdom persuaded many people that wilderness areas, such as the Sierra Nevada Mountains, should be valued and preserved because beauty is essential to the human spirit.

The majority of those opposing the conservation movement wished to profit from the land rather than conserve it. Logging companies cut down forests to sell lumber, and builders constructed hotels and houses with the lumber. Mining companies stripped mountains of their trees and soil to extract the valuable minerals

According to writer and philosopher Henry David Thoreau (1817-1862), "In wildness is the preservation of the world." Thoreau's love of nature and criticism of overdevelopment influenced many environmentalists, including John Muir and Aldo Leopold.

underneath. Gun manufacturers and sporting companies encouraged customers to shoot big game like grizzly bears and mountain lions, bringing these animals to near extinction. Farmers and ranchers used and often abused *federal lands*—lands held by the government for everyone's use—to feed their livestock. Because their commercial ventures provided jobs and goods for the large number of people who were settling in the West, these entrepreneurs could not understand why a beautiful valley or a mountain lion should be preserved instead of being used to make money.

In 1872, the U.S. government established the nation's first national park, Yellowstone, which lies in three states: Wyoming, Idaho, and Montana. A *national park* is an area of scenic beauty or historical importance that is owned and maintained by the government for use by the people. The government designated Yellowstone as a national park to protect the area's natural hot springs that sporadically spurt geysers of water and steam into the air. The crush of commercialism had already marred such other natural wonders as Niagara Falls in New York.

The establishment of Yellowstone National Park was the first successful campaign of the early conservation movement. The movement made further progress when Theodore Roosevelt, called the first conservation president, assumed office in 1901. In one address to Congress he said:

> It would be utterly wrong to allow a few individuals to exhaust for their own temporary personal profit the resources which ought to be developed through use so as to be conserved for the common advantage of the people as a whole.

By the time Roosevelt left office in 1909, he had preserved 18 *national monuments* (historic sites or important geographic areas) and 51 *national wildlife refuges* (areas protected as sanctuaries for wildlife, primarily waterfowl and migratory birds). He also designated 100 million acres as national forests. A *national forest* is forested land owned, maintained, and preserved by the U.S. government. Without federal protection, many of America's magnificent wildlands would have been destroyed by development.

President Theodore Roosevelt (left) often consulted with Gifford Pinchot (1865-1946), head of what became the U.S. Forest Service, regarding conservation policies. Pinchot's belief in the wise use of natural resources was sometimes at odds with conservationists such as John Muir, who wanted to preserve some areas from any development.

Well-known landscape photographer William Henry Jackson (1843-1942) took this photograph of the Great Falls of the Yellowstone River in 1872, the year the area became the nation's first national park. Jackson worked as the official photographer for the U.S. Geological Survey of the Territories between 1870 and 1878.

13

In 1892, John Muir founded the Sierra Club, the first national conservation organization. The group's efforts culminated in the passage of the National Park Organic Act of 1916 (commonly known as the National Park Service Act). That act stated that the purpose of national parks and monuments was "to conserve the scenery and the natural and historic objects and wildlife therein and to provide for the enjoyment of the same in such manner and by such means as will leave them unimpaired for the enjoyment of future generations."

For the next several decades, conservationists focused their efforts on halting the decline of the wildlife populations that were not protected by the National Park Organic Act. In January 1905, Audubon Societies in 36 states established the National Association of Audubon Societies for the Protection of Wild Birds and Animals. But 25 years later, the organization would begin to lose sight of its original goals, and Rosalie Edge would play a pivotal role in setting it back on track.

Between 1930 and 1934, the autumn migration of waterfowl in the United States plunged from an estimated 100 million to 20 million ducks. While chief of the U.S. Bureau of Biological Survey (BBS), J. N. "Ding" Darling mounted a successful effort to enlarge the National Wildlife Refuge System so that the remaining birds and their habitats were protected.

Forester Aldo Leopold and field biologist Olaus Murie both personally witnessed loss of wildlife caused by overgrazing and overlogging. In the late 1930s and early 1940s, they recommended that the U.S. government oversee the use of national lands for the benefit of all living things, not just people. "When we see land as a community to which we belong," wrote Leopold, "we may begin to use it with love and respect." In January 1935, Leopold and Murie joined Robert Marshall (also a U.S. forester and a wilderness advocate) and others to found The Wilderness Society, an organization dedicated

Aldo Leopold (left) and Olaus Murie, shown here in 1946, helped to organize The Wilderness Society.

to protecting America's wildlands. They believed that land should be used to benefit the entire environment and that the importance of a particular area to *all* species—human, plant, and animal—must be considered.

Following World War II, thousands of new homes were constructed for returning veterans and their families. More automobiles were made and driven without thought to the large amounts of gasoline they burned or the air pollution caused by their engine exhaust. People poisoned the environment by using pesticides to kill backyard insects. The conservation movement now entered another phase, focusing on more than simply conserving the nation's natural resources and wildlife. Now called environmentalists, the successors to the earlier conservationists sought to protect the whole earth and all of its inhabitants from the increasing problems of air and water pollution, toxic pesticides, and other industrial hazards in the twentieth century.

In her revolutionary book *Silent Spring*, published in 1962, Rachel Carson issued this warning about unregulated pesticide use: "For the first time in the history of the world, every human being is now subjected to contact with dangerous chemicals, from the moment of conception until death." As a result of *Silent Spring*, the U.S. Congress banned the pesticide DDT and other harmful chemicals. In addition, Carson's book alerted many people to the need for regulating all activities having the potential to harm the environment.

This photograph of the Los Angeles area taken in 1962 illustrates the urban sprawl that has affected the quality of the environment.

In 1964, Congress passed the landmark Wilderness Act, establishing the National Wilderness Preservation System. The act described wilderness as "an area where the earth and its community of life are untrammeled" by human beings. Wilderness, the act continued, is a place where a person is "a visitor who does not remain."

Margaret Murie (third from left) watches President Lyndon Johnson sign the Wilderness Act into law.

Six years later, in 1970, Senator Gaylord Nelson of Wisconsin began Earth Day, which is celebrated in the United States on April 22. This special day reminds all citizens that if planet Earth is to survive, they must give precedence to the protection of the environment. As a direct result of Earth Day, Congress passed amendments strengthening the Clean Air and Clean Water Acts.

By this time, *grassroots* efforts—actions by ordinary citizens on the local level to influence the decisions being made by big business and politicians—were becoming widespread in the United States. Protesters carried signs opposing unpopular congressional bills and gathered signatures for petitions against environmental damage caused by acid rain, oil spills, and nuclear power. They *boycotted*, or refused to do business with, companies selling environmentally harmful products. Through these efforts, ordinary citizens were forcing businesses and politicians to listen to what they had to say.

At the close of the twentieth century, most people believe that a safe and healthy environment should be a political priority. According to a 1990 poll, 74 percent of the respondents believed that "protecting the environment is so important that requirements and standards cannot be too high, and continuing environmental improvements must be made regardless of cost."

The following chapters tell the stories of nine women and men who have helped to bring our world to this new dedication to the principles of conservation.

Many people have embraced the new three "R's"— reduce, reuse, recycle—making recycling bins such as this one common curbside sights.

John Muir (1838-1914) once said, "Everybody needs beauty as well as bread." He spent most of his adult life exploring, writing about, and fighting to protect Yosemite and other areas of natural beauty in the western United States.

1

John Muir
Man of the Mountains

*D*aniel Muir, a strict, fanatically religious man, wanted his eight children only to pray and work. He allowed no other activity. To rest for the next day's work, they went to bed early. One evening, John Muir stayed up to read after the family's evening worship. Daniel told his teenage son that he had to go to bed when everyone else did. "If you *will* read," he told John, "do it in the morning. You may get up as early as you like."

John Muir took advantage of this rare concession by getting up sometimes as early as 1 A.M. to read or to tinker with his inventions in the freezing cold cellar. To make getting up easier, he invented an "early rising machine." He connected a clock to a crossbeam supporting the bed, that, at a preset hour, would tilt the bed and dump John onto the floor! This private time was immensely important to him. "Five hours to myself!" he exulted, "five huge, solid hours!"

John Muir, the father of the American conservation movement, was born in Dunbar, Scotland, on April 21, 1838, the third child of Daniel Muir and Ann (or Anne in some sources) Gilrye Muir. During his early school years in Scotland, students were whipped if they did not know their lessons. John was also beaten at home by his father if he failed to memorize a verse from the Bible every day. At the time, many people thought that physical punishment was both appropriate and necessary for raising children.

In his free time, John also went on "scootchers," or expeditions, with his friends. They explored the seashore, staged battles in Dunbar castle, or stole fruit from orchards. He and his younger brother David also enjoyed spending evenings with their grandparents. They were with the Gilryes when Daniel Muir announced that the boys did not have to study their lessons that night. "We're going to America in the morning," their father informed them.

In a quest to find a religion that met his rigid standards, Daniel Muir had joined the Disciples of Christ, a group determined to practice the early Christianity of the apostles. When the Disciples took their mission to North America, Muir decided to join them.

On February 19, 1849, Muir and three of his children—John, David, and one of their older sisters, Sarah—left for America. They settled in the wilderness of southeast Wisconsin, near Portage. Before they could plant crops, the trees and roots and boulders that covered their property had to be removed. Eleven-year-old John was barely able to reach the top of the plow when his father put him behind an ox and told him to clear a field. Muir had a large home built, and his wife and the other four children joined the family before winter. The eighth Muir child, Joanna, was born in Wisconsin.

John had to help on the farm instead of attending school. But he borrowed books from neighbors to read and taught himself algebra, geometry, and trigonometry. In the summer of 1860, at age 22, John Muir took his inventions to the state fair in Madison, where they won prizes and praise. Muir worked in Madison until he enrolled at the University of Wisconsin in February 1861.

At the university, Muir studied botany and chemistry. Professor Ezra Carr introduced him to geology, and Carr's wife, Jeanne, became Muir's mentor and friend. After two years, Muir journeyed to Canada, possibly to avoid being drafted to fight in the Civil War. Traveling lightly, he jotted down notes about the plants and wildlife he saw, as well as his thoughts about the relationship between humans and nature.

John Muir's drawing of the desk he invented while a student at the University of Wisconsin. A timer, set for a specified period of study, could close up one textbook and then move another to the desktop and open it.

After months of wandering the woods on his own, Muir joined his brother, Daniel Jr. They worked in a sawmill in Meaford, Ontario, until the mill burned down. In 1866, Muir settled in Indianapolis, Indiana, where his mechanical talents enabled him to find work in a carriage factory.

One evening in March 1867, an event occurred that changed Muir's life forever. While he was fixing a machine belt, a metal file flew from his hand and pierced the cornea of his right eye. The *aqueous humor*, the liquid that protects and lubricates the eyes, flowed out, blinding him.

Within a few days, Muir also lost the sight in his left eye from nervous shock. His friends consulted an eye specialist who thought that Muir's sight would return if he would lie quietly for several weeks while his damaged eye refilled with fluid. Muir did as he was instructed, but he was in great physical and mental pain. "My days were terrible beyond what I can tell," he wrote later, "and my nights were, if possible, more terrible. Frightful dreams exhausted and terrified me." During his ordeal, Muir considered how he wanted to spend the rest of his life.

Slowly, sight returned to both of Muir's eyes, a healing process that he compared to a religious experience. Instead of working with machines and inventing new ones, Muir decided to spend the rest of his life studying "the inventions of God."

With a press to dry and preserve plant specimens and a few favorite books, John Muir set out in 1867 on a thousand-mile walk through the southern United States to the Gulf of Mexico. From there, he planned to travel on to South America. In his journal, he wrote his observations of the weather, the topographical features of the land, and the different plant and animal species he came across. He also jotted down notes about the human inhabitants he met. His journal, *A Thousand-Mile Walk to the Gulf*, would not be published until 1916.

While traveling in Florida, Muir contracted malaria. Still weak and feverish when he arrived in Havana, Cuba, he realized that he was not strong enough to continue his journey to South America. Muir boarded a ship to San Francisco, hoping that the cool mountain air in the West might cure him.

When he arrived in San Francisco on March 28, 1868, the weary Muir asked someone the fastest way out of town—to anywhere "that is wild." The stranger pointed him east, in the direction of the Sierra Nevada Mountains. After traveling across central California, John Muir reached the mountains and Yosemite Valley. He felt that he had come home.

After 10 days in Yosemite, Muir went to the San Joaquin Valley, where he worked odd jobs. That winter, Muir was a shepherd. But he soon developed a dislike for sheep, which he called "hooved locusts" because their sharp hoofs tore up the ground underneath. In the spring of 1869, Muir herded his sheep into the mountains surrounding Yosemite and spent the summer there. In the autumn, he began sawing lumber for James Hutchings, a hotel owner who wanted to build more cottages for Yosemite visitors. Muir accepted the job with the understanding that he would work only on trees that had been blown down by the wind—not cut down by loggers.

John Muir loathed the damage to the grasses and wildflowers inflicted by "hooved locusts," or sheep, such as this herd grazing in Tuolumne Meadows in northeastern Yosemite.

When he wasn't working, Muir was free to do whatever he wished and to go wherever he pleased. What pleased him most was wandering through Yosemite Valley sketching, writing, and observing. In his words, he would "throw some tea and bread in an old sack and jump over the back fence."

27

This photograph of John Muir was taken shortly after he arrived in San Francisco at the age of 30.

Yosemite was becoming popular with tourists—and so was John Muir, who often acted as a guide for the guests of Hutchings's hotel. His knowledge of the area gained him a reputation as a colorful mountain "character" who knew more about the Sierra Nevada than the trained *geologists*, scientists who study the structure of the earth. Many famous people of the time, including philosopher-writer Ralph Waldo Emerson, sought out "John of the Mountains," as he was known. Ezra Carr, Muir's former professor at the University of Wisconsin, was now living in California, and he and his wife encouraged people to visit Muir.

It was with Carr that Muir first discussed his theory that Yosemite had been formed by glaciers and not by an enormous earthquake, which was a popular theory at the time. Muir had found the remnants of a glacier at Yosemite and measured its movement. Encouraged by Carr, John Muir sent an article about his glacier theory to the *New York Tribune*, which published the piece in December 1871. Today, most scientists agree that glaciers and rivers carved out the spectacular Yosemite Valley.

John Muir found a spiritual home in the wilds of Yosemite, such as this beautiful spot on the Merced River with Half Dome towering in the distance.

In 1874, a series of articles by John Muir called "Sierra Studies" appeared in *Overland Monthly*. Now Muir traveled and explored during the summer and wrote articles while living with friends in San Francisco in the winter. During one stay in the city, the Carrs introduced Muir to Louie Wanda Strentzel. The two married in April 1880. They took over the Strentzel family fruit farm, across the bay from San Francisco. Their two daughters, Annie Wanda and Helen, were born there.

For most of the next decade, Muir devoted his time to the orchards. His hard work and natural talent for horticulture resulted in a successful business—so successful that in 1888 he sold part of the land and leased the rest. The decision to sell came partly at the insistence of his wife, who worried that the stress of running the farm and the long separation from his beloved wilderness were ruining her husband's health and spirit.

In 1889, Muir took his friend Robert Underwood Johnson, the editor of *Century* magazine, on a camping trip in the mountains. Muir hoped that what Johnson saw—land damaged by overgrazing sheep and forests depleted by excessive logging—would shock him into some kind of action. Johnson, in turn, hoped to convince Muir to begin writing again. Both men accomplished their goals.

Together, Johnson and Muir launched a campaign to protect Yosemite Valley. They wanted the federal government to make the land surrounding Yosemite a national park. At the time, there was only one national park in the United States—Yellowstone.

Muir's articles, "Treasures of the Yosemite" and "Features of the Proposed Yosemite National Park," informed the American public about the threats to Yosemite and urged people to support its protection as a national park. He also wrote letters to California newspapers and gave interviews and talks exposing Yosemite's deteriorating condition.

Johnson published Muir's articles in *Century* and promoted the national park proposal in his editorials. He

Century *magazine was at the height of its success and influence when editor Robert Underwood Johnson (1853-1937) and John Muir campaigned for Yosemite to become a national park. Johnson published work by some of the best writers of the day, including Mark Twain and Henry James.*

called on political friends in Washington, D.C., to support and publicize the proposed park. The task that Muir and Johnson had taken on was not an easy one, but they were successful. The public responded by contacting their representatives in Congress and demanding protection for Yosemite. In 1890, Congress bowed to public pressure and designated Yosemite as the nation's second national park.

On May 28, 1892, Muir founded the Sierra Club, one of the first environmental organizations in the United States, and served as the group's first president. One of the club's stated goals was "to enlist the support and cooperation of the people and the government in preserving the forests and other natural features of the Sierra Nevada." An early conservation campaign conducted by the Sierra Club resulted in the U.S. Senate defeating a bill supported by western loggers and ranchers that would have cut Yosemite National Park in half.

The momentum created by this successful Yosemite campaign—which many people believe marked the beginning of the modern environmental movement—led to the passage of other conservation bills in the 1890s. Before leaving office in 1893, President Benjamin Harrison had created 15 forest reserves—later called national forests—that totaled 13 million acres. Three years later, his successor, President Grover Cleveland, created the Forestry Commission, on which John Muir served as an adviser. Based on the findings of the commission's report, Cleveland set aside 13 new forest reserves, consisting of 21 million acres.

Timber companies that had been selling logs cut in the newly created forest reserves were not happy with Cleveland's action. To give them time to cut down more trees, they pressured Congress to withdraw the "forest reserve" status until March 1, 1898.

Muir responded by writing several articles about the issue, including "The American Forests" for the *Atlantic Monthly*, which stated:

> Any fool can destroy trees. They cannot run away; and if they could, they would still be destroyed,—chased and hunted down as long as fun or a dollar could be got out of their bark hides. . . . Through all the wonderful, eventful centuries since Christ's time—and long before that— God has cared for these trees, saved them from drought, disease, avalanches, and a thousand straining, leveling tempests and floods; but he cannot save them from fools,—only Uncle Sam can do that.

Once again, Muir succeeded in rousing the public to action, and Congress restored the forest reserves.

In 1903, President Theodore Roosevelt asked Muir to take him on a camping trip to Yosemite: "I want to drop politics absolutely for four days," wrote the president, "and just be out in the open with you." During the trip, Muir talked to Roosevelt about the threats to wilderness and the importance of wild areas to the human spirit and to the nation as a whole. Muir told Roosevelt

Theodore Roosevelt (1858-1919) and John Muir stand on Glacier Point during their camping trip. One night, while the two slept under the sky, several inches of snow fell. Roosevelt was delighted to wake up and find himself covered with the spring snow.

that as president he could help to stop the degradation of America's public lands by declaring his support for more national parks and forest reserves.

Before Theodore Roosevelt left office in 1909, he added more than 100,000 acres to the forest reserves and pressured Congress into creating 6 new national parks and 53 wildlife reserves, later called wildlife refuges. In 1906, he convinced Congress to pass the Lacey Antiquities Act, which gave the president authority to create national monuments by proclamation. Roosevelt then created 16 national monuments, among them the Muir Woods National Monument in California.

But John Muir also experienced defeat and, sadly, lost the battle that meant the most to him. San Francisco city officials proposed building a dam in the Hetch Hetchy Valley in the northwest corner of Yosemite National Park. They said the dam was necessary to provide water and power for the city.

Muir, however, maintained that Hetch Hetchy Valley was "one of Nature's rarest and most precious mountain temples." He opposed the proposal because he feared that a dam in a national park would not only flood the valley, but would also undermine the ideals for which the parks were protected in the first place.

In 1913, despite nationwide protests, Congress voted to go ahead with building the dam. It was a bitter blow to the 75-year-old Muir. Yet he did not lose hope for the future because "the battle for conservation will go on

Photographer Joseph Le Conte captured the lush beauty of Hetch Hetchy Valley (above) before the dam was constructed. The photograph below shows the same spot completely flooded after the dam was built.

endlessly. It is part of the universal warfare between right and wrong," he stated.

Despite their defeat, the team of conservationists, railroad officials, and tourism promoters that Muir had assembled to fight the Hetch Hetchy Dam continued to work together. Three years later, in 1916, they influenced Congress to create the National Park Service, an agency dedicated to overseeing and protecting national parks like Yosemite. The Service's first director was Sierra Club member Stephen Mather. Sadly, John Muir, who is often called the father of our national parks, did not live to see this victory. He had died of pneumonia on Christmas Eve in 1914.

Today, John Muir's work and words still inspire and influence the environmental movement. More than 100 years since it began, the Sierra Club boasts a membership of 550,000 and continues to lobby for government policies favorable to the environment. Its legal team fights in the courts to enforce the laws that have already been made to protect the earth, and its publishing division produces books about the environment. The Sierra Club also sponsors outdoor adventures that would have delighted John Muir.

More than 3 million people visit Yosemite each year, taking Muir's advice to "climb the mountains and get their good tidings." Ironically, overuse of this beautiful place is the greatest challenge Yosemite faces today.

Jay Norwood "Ding" Darling (1876-1962) at his drawing board, sketching the ducks he loved and worked so hard to save

2

Jay Norwood "Ding" Darling
Cartoonist and Conservationist

*T*he signs marking the boundaries in every national wildlife refuge feature a picture of a flying goose. The designer of this insignia, J. N. "Ding" Darling, was a nationally syndicated political cartoonist. As head of the Bureau for Biological Survey in the mid-1930s, he was also the person most responsible for enlarging America's wildlife refuge system. Today, the refuge system includes more than 500 sanctuaries for wildlife and natural habitat.

Jay Norwood Darling was born on October 21, 1876, to Marcellus W. Darling, a Methodist minister, and

Clara Woolson Darling. His middle name came from his birthplace of Norwood, Michigan. Marc Darling served several churches in Michigan and Indiana before being transferred to Sioux City, Iowa, in 1886. There Jay and his brother, Frank, roamed the prairies and explored the Missouri and Big Sioux Rivers. Jay also spent several summers working on his uncle's farm in Albion, Michigan. He later herded cattle in South Dakota. Through these experiences, Jay learned to love the outdoors and nature. Looking back on the lands he loved in those years, he would write, "If I could put together all the virgin landscapes which I knew in my youth and show what has happened to them in one generation it would be the best object lesson in conservation."

In 1894, Darling began his college career at Yankton College in South Dakota, but he was expelled the following year after "borrowing" the president's horse and buggy. His sense of humor also got him into trouble during his second stab at collegiate life at Beloit College in Wisconsin. From a young age, Darling had demonstrated a talent for writing and drawing, and he put these skills to use as the art director of the Beloit yearbook. One day, he decided to liven things up a bit by drawing caricatures of some of his professors. He signed the cartoons "D'ing." Darling explained, "The apostrophe stood for the 'arl,' which were left out in order to make a funnier looking signature and in addition to conceal my identity."

The concealment did not work, but his cartoons were not the only reason Beloit officials suspended Darling. They cited "irregularities in attendance and poor scholarship" because he was failing nearly every course. Nevertheless, Darling rallied from this setback and graduated from Beloit in 1900. For the rest of his life, he signed his name "Ding Darling" without the apostrophe.

Although Darling wanted to go to medical school, economics dictated that he earn some money instead. His first job following graduation was as a reporter for the *Sioux City Journal.* Soon he was spicing up his articles with sketches and cartoons. In 1906, he married Genevieve Pendleton, known as Penny. While they were on their honeymoon, the *Des Moines Register and Leader* (later the *Des Moines Register*) telegraphed a job offer to Darling. He accepted.

At his new job at the *Register,* Darling began using cartoons to voice his environmental concerns. His very first cartoon, showing a monk smoking "soft coal" in a pipe, implied that soft coal was the reason for Des Moines's air pollution. His other cartoons commented on land erosion, water pollution, and overpopulation.

Before long, Darling's sketches became so popular he gave up writing altogether. An avid duck hunter himself, he often criticized hunters who ignored hunting seasons or shot more ducks than allowed by law. One of these duck-hunting cartoons caught the attention of the publishers of the *New York Herald Tribune.* In 1916, this noted newspaper began to *syndicate*, or sell to other newspapers, Darling's sketches.

Eventually, 300 newspapers across the country featured Ding Darling's cartoons. In 1924, he won a Pulitzer Prize for cartooning. With this honor, an annual award given for outstanding works in American journalism, literature, and music, Darling had achieved a national reputation. Throughout the United States, people praised him as a political cartoonist and as an activist who wanted to protect wildlife and land.

Darling had long been involved in efforts to reform Iowa's conservation policies, especially those dealing with wildlife. In 1931, he persuaded the Iowa state legislature to create the State Fish and Game Commission. The commission would set policies for and monitor the management of the state's natural resources. One year later, Darling became one of the new organization's first commissioners.

The national conservation scene also received Ding Darling's attention. As a hunter, he had witnessed firsthand the rapid decline in populations of wildlife, particularly waterfowl. In 1930, an estimated 100 million ducks crossed the skies in their annual autumn flights south across the United States. According to annual bird counts taken only a few years later, that number had dropped to an estimated 20 million—a net loss of 80 million birds in only four years.

Without wetlands such as these, ducks and other water birds have no place to live, feed, raise their young, or rest during migration.

What had happened to the ducks? The U.S. government had enacted a program to drain millions of acres of wetlands to create more farmland. These *wetlands*, areas saturated with water such as marshes and swamps, were important breeding places for waterfowl. After drainage, Darling later wrote, the marshes "had nothing on them but cockleburs and bankrupt farmers." A 10-year-long drought had worsened the situation, leaving the central Great Plains dry and largely barren.

The U.S. Bureau of Biological Survey (BBS), an agency of the Department of Agriculture, was in charge of managing wildfowl on public lands. To prevent further loss of wildlife, conservationists suggested that the bureau shorten the hunting season and lower *bag limits*—the number of birds a hunter could shoot each day. The bag limit was cut from 25 to 15 birds a day, but waterfowl populations continued to decline.

Darling, a staunch Republican, normally criticized the lack of conservation efforts by Democratic President Franklin Delano Roosevelt's administration. But, primarily because of his friendship with Secretary of Agriculture Henry Wallace, a fellow Iowan, Darling restrained his censure of the federal government's wildlife policies and recommended only that the BBS direct its resources toward restoring and maintaining wildlife habitats rather than merely regulating and policing them.

Darling's silence was rewarded in January 1934 when Roosevelt appointed him to serve on the President's Committee on Wild-Life Restoration. The committee was to devise a plan to save the waterfowl population. The two other members, Aldo Leopold and Thomas Beck, who was named the committee's chair, were also enthusiastic duck hunters. A former U.S. forester, Leopold was the first professor of wildlife management at the University of Wisconsin. Beck edited a popular magazine and was chair of the Connecticut State Board of Fisheries and Game.

*President Franklin D. Roosevelt (1882-1945) left,
and his secretary of agriculture, Henry Wallace
(1888-1965). Wallace oversaw the agency in charge
of wildlife management on federal lands. An effective
and intelligent administrator, Wallace later served as
Roosevelt's vice-president from 1941 to 1945.*

The three committee members began their work
on January 8, 1934, with enthusiasm and optimism but
without the cooperation of the Bureau of Biological
Survey staff, who felt they needed no outside help. The
committee worked hard—and fast—and released its
report on February 6, 1934, less than a month later. The
report emphasized the need to restore the ducks' nesting
areas and recommended that the government buy several million acres of marginal farmland and turn it into

new wildlife refuges. Ironically, the lands the committee recommended purchasing were often the former wetlands the government had previously drained.

The federal government would need $50 to $75 million to buy these lands. Creating a federal duck stamp was one of the suggestions for raising the funds. Each duck-hunting season, hunters would pay $1 for the stamp on their license to hunt migratory game birds. The government would use the proceeds from the sale of these stamps to purchase and maintain wildlife refuges. The committee also suggested that the government raise funds by placing a tax on the sale of firearms and ammunition.

While both conservationists and hunters praised the report, President Franklin D. Roosevelt did not respond. Frustrated because the committee's efforts seemed to have been in vain, Darling began to attack Roosevelt's wildlife policies. Irritated himself by the criticism, the president offered Darling the post of chief of the Bureau of Biological Survey. Darling accepted the job reluctantly, agreeing to serve only temporarily.

Despite his short tenure with the BBS, Darling's work made an impact. He reorganized the agency and created the Migratory Waterfowl Division. This division became responsible for policy decisions and for the management of all wildlife refuges except those for large mammals. The division also conducted field studies of potential refuges and worked with the government real-estate office to acquire refuge lands.

This Ding Darling cartoon, "Nobody's Constituents," illustrated his reason for accepting the position of chief of the Bureau of Biological Survey.

Once sworn in, Darling began working to implement the Migratory Bird Hunting Stamp Act of 1934, or the Duck Stamp Act, which had been signed into law a few days before he took office. One day Darling sat at a lunchroom table and drew on a brown paper bag the very first duck stamp—a pair of mallards landing on a marsh. The act turned out to be one of the most famous conservation programs in the history of the United States. Since 1935, the duck stamp program has funded the preservation of 4 million acres of wildlife habitat.

Ding Darling not only administered the Migratory Bird Hunting Stamp Act of 1934, he also drew this pair of mallards for the first federal "duck stamp."

Perhaps Darling's most important contribution while serving as head of the Bureau of Biological Survey was the enormous sum of money he garnered almost single-handedly to bolster the struggling refuge system. When he took the job as chief of the BBS, Darling called wildlife the government's "orphan child, without asylum, that has subsisted on the crumbs the neighbors sent in." He did not hesitate to ask those "neighbors" for more crumbs, often trekking from agency to agency requesting donations of unused money.

One of his colleagues at the *Des Moines Register* called Darling "an extreme extrovert, awed by nobody, overflowing with self-confidence." Those traits served him well as he took on the task of funding the refuges, once admitting that he used "a straw to suck funds from the other fellow's barrel."

To support his requests, he presented letters of authorization from President Roosevelt. On memo pads he called chits, the president had written to Secretary Wallace, Darling's boss: "Dear Henry, please find a million dollars among some of your funds which Ding can use for the conservation of his ducks." While most of the governmental agencies did not give the chits much credence—as the president knew they would not—some did respond, including the Drought Relief Fund and the Works Progress Administration. Using this strategy, Darling was able to raise $2.5 million for the purchase of land for new refuges.

Not focused solely on wildlife management, Ding Darling was also concerned about air and water pollution, overpopulation, and erosion.

Next, Darling convinced Congress to appropriate another $6 million to the BBS. And the following year, he asked President Roosevelt for $4 million more:

> We can make better use of retired agricultural land than anybody. Others grow grass and trees on it. We grow grass, trees, marshes, lakes, ducks, geese, fur-bearers, impounded water and recreation. . . . We did a good job last year. Why cut us off now?

Although the president turned Darling down, good-naturedly accusing him of robbing the U.S. Treasury, Darling's efforts had helped to add more than 900,000 acres to the National Wildlife Refuge System.

After leading the BBS for almost two years, Darling began to tire of the bickering and the difficulty in getting results. What finally pushed him out the door was a government decision on a proposal by several gun companies. These companies offered to raise a $10 million endowment fund for wildlife protection in exchange for an end to the government's tax on guns and ammunition. Taxes on the sale of guns and ammunition raised the price that customers had to pay, which resulted in fewer purchases. The manufacturers felt that donating $10 million to protect wildlife would be a good investment for them because it would result in more animals for sport hunters who, in turn, would likely buy more guns and ammunition to shoot the animals. Roosevelt's administration turned down their proposal.

Darling favored the idea and called this rejection "more than my placid disposition can accept." In September 1935, with his usual good humor and grace, Darling resigned his position. He left the BBS convinced that conservationists needed to be as organized as the commercial interests that exploited natural resources.

With that goal in mind, he founded the General Wildlife Federation in 1936 and served as its president from 1936 until 1939. Although Darling complained that the group never accomplished its purpose of coordinating the many different state and local conservation organizations, the federation evolved into the National Wildlife Federation. Today, the goal of this organization of 4 million members is to "educate, inspire, and assist" people in conserving wildlife and natural resources through its many educational programs for children and young adults. Ding Darling, who came to believe that principles of conservation should be taught in the schools, would have approved of its approach.

Darling returned to the *Des Moines Register* and won his second Pulitzer Prize for cartooning in 1942. He retired from the newspaper in 1949, but he continued his conservation work. For example, while cruising through the Florida Keys in 1952, he saw hunters set fire to an island to flush out the small Key deer from the woods to the beaches, where the hunters would then slaughter them. His sketch of the hunt generated public support for the Key Deer Refuge Bill, which was passed in 1957. Darling and Walt Disney were named cochairmen of National Wildlife Week in 1962, but Ding Darling died on February 12, shortly before the observance was to take place.

After his death, 60 of his colleagues, admirers, and friends established the J. N. "Ding" Darling Foundation. As its first project, the foundation promoted one of Darling's ideas—the Lewis and Clark Trail, a historical trail that follows the route of the famous explorers from

St. Joseph, Missouri, to the Pacific Coast. The U.S. Congress established the trail system in 1964, and several Darling foundation members were appointed to the commission that oversees the trail. In 1967, then Secretary of the Interior Stewart Udall renamed the Sanibel Island Refuge on the west coast of Florida—one of Darling's favorite bird-watching sites—the J. N. "Ding" Darling National Wildlife Refuge.

Today, Darling's work as a cartoonist and conservationist is visible to visitors at any national wildlife refuge. The flying-goose insignia on the refuge signs was drawn by Darling. More important, Darling expanded the boundary lines of many of these sanctuaries where wildlife and plants have a place to live and grow.

Mabel Rosalie Barrow Edge (1877-1962) loved birds and spent the last 33 years of her life protecting them and their habitats.

3

Rosalie Edge
For the Birds

*R*osalie Edge, the first woman to have a real impact on the American conservation movement, was already middle-aged when she began to work on environmental issues. Her environmental career was launched one evening during the summer of 1929 when she was in Paris. Just before leaving her hotel room to join her family for dinner, she picked up a pamphlet entitled "A Crisis in Conservation," which had arrived in the mail.

Written by Willard Van Name, a scientist at the American Museum of Natural History, the pamphlet accused a well-funded bird-protection association of receiving money from gun manufacturers. The organization, charged Van Name, performed its work with "inertia, incompetency and procrastination." Although he did not disclose the name of this group, Van Name was clearly referring to the National Association of Audubon Societies (now called the National Audubon Society), an American organization founded to protect wild birds.

The pamphlet greatly upset Edge, a lifetime Audubon member and a fervent bird lover. In fact, it so perturbed her that she forgot to join her family for dinner. She had no time for restaurants and the Paris scene when her mind, she wrote later, "was filled with the tragedy of beautiful birds, disappearing through the neglect and indifference of those who had at their disposal wealth beyond avarice with which these creatures might be saved." She vowed to do something about the situation as soon as she returned to New York. At the age of 52, Rosalie Edge was about to become "the only honest, unselfish, indomitable hellcat in the history of conservation," as Willard Van Name would later describe her.

Mabel Rosalie Barrow was raised to be a lady, not a hellcat. Born on November 3, 1877, into a wealthy New York City family, she attended Manhattan finishing schools with other young women of her social class. In 1909, she married Charles Noel Edge, a British consulting engineer. For a while, the couple lived overseas, but they returned to the United States in 1913. On the trip home, Rosalie Edge met Lady Margaret Rhondda, a British suffragette and publisher who inspired Edge's own involvement in the movement to gain voting rights for women. "It was the first awakening of my mind," Edge later recalled.

Edge spent the next seven years immersed in the effort to obtain women's right to vote. She served as secretary of the New York State Woman's Suffrage Party, and a plaque commemorating her work hangs in the Albany State House. (The Nineteenth Amendment to the U.S. Constitution, granting women the right to vote, became law in August 1920.) The experience she gained during her suffragist campaign—making public speeches, raising money, and working with the press—prepared her for her later work on behalf of the environment.

During the time she worked for the women's suffrage movement, Rosalie Edge also became an enthusiastic bird watcher and joined the National Audubon Society. Her life list of bird species observed totaled 804. Once when she was late to a suffrage meeting, she explained that she had been watching a great blue heron in her maple tree.

When Edge returned from her 1929 trip to Paris, she immediately began to study the policies of the Audubon Society. At the organization's annual meeting that autumn, she stood up, waved a copy of Willard Van Name's pamphlet at the Audubon officials, and demanded to know if the charges were true. She particularly wanted

Named for wildlife painter John James Audubon (1785-1851, right), the first Audubon Society was founded in 1886 by George Bird Grinnell. Members worked to protect nongame birds, such as this sparrow hawk (left), that were being shot mainly for their feathers.

to know if Gilbert Pearson, the organization's president, was more interested in keeping gun companies happy than in protecting waterfowl. (At that time, the Audubon Society rarely took a stand on protecting game birds.)

A shocked silence descended on the meeting. Pearson's response to the charges was vague and unsatisfactory. He later complained that Edge "had spoiled the meeting" because she left them with no time "to show the motion picture which was to have been the feature of the morning."

Soon afterward, Edge joined forces with Willard Van Name and Irving Brant, a journalist and nature lover who also was critical of both the Audubon Society and Gilbert Pearson. He had heard about Edge's disruption of the 1929 meeting.

Determined to reform the Audubon Society, Edge, Brant, and Van Name teamed up to establish the Emergency Conservation Committee (ECC). Over the years, the ECC evolved into an organization that took on other environmental issues as well. The three worked out of a tiny office with limited funds, provided primarily by Edge, who took no salary during the 32 years she headed

Scientist Willard Van Name cofounded the Emergency Conservation Committee with Rosalie Edge and Irving Brant.

the organization. The three leaders employed tactics that Edge had learned in the suffragist movement: "create news and reform from within."

Prior to the Audubon Society's 1930 annual meeting, Edge mailed a pamphlet entitled "Compromised Conservation" to newspapers and to organizations interested in wildlife. The pamphlet revealed the Audubon Society's connections with sport hunters and gun manufacturers and accused Gilbert Pearson of hoarding surplus Audubon funds instead of spending the money on programs to protect birds. She claimed that Pearson did this because he received a percentage of the organization's annual income instead of a fixed salary.

Edge also enlisted the aid of zoologist William Hornaday, who joined the National Audubon Society so he would be allowed to speak at the meeting. Hornaday believed that the organization had neglected the bird population except for its value as game for sport hunters. According to Hornaday:

> For too long have American bird conservationists been humbly meandering along behind the firing lines, picking up the cripples. To be sure, they are trying to "save" them. They gather up the fragments of wildlife, "band" it for reference purposes or pen it up and try to induce it to lay eggs and breed more gunfodder birds, for more shooting by more sportsmen and more crops of cripples.

At the 1930 annual meeting, Edge demanded that the board of directors investigate her charges against

Director of the New York Zoological Park, William Temple Hornaday (1854-1937) was a respected wildlife conservation leader. His 1887 book, Extermination of the American Bison, *had helped to save the bison from extinction.*

Pearson. To placate her, the Audubon board appointed a three-person investigative committee. The committee publicly cleared Pearson of any wrongdoing, calling his critics a self-appointed "zoophile cult." Privately, however, the board later wrote a confidential report—not released to the public—in which they placed a tighter control on Pearson's activities and paid him a fixed salary.

Several days after the 1930 meeting, Edge asked Pearson for a copy of the Audubon Society's membership list. When he refused, Edge brought a lawsuit against the Audubon Society. She won the case, but not before one of the Audubon lawyers scornfully called her a "common scold." More amused than offended by the remark, Edge laughed and said, "Fancy how I trembled."

Once Rosalie Edge had the list of Audubon members, she sent a letter to each of them asking for their *proxies* (written permission to use their vote) at the next annual meeting. She also sent them a pamphlet accusing the Audubon Society of approving the trapping of wild animals in the Rainey Wildlife Sanctuary in Louisiana and then profiting from the sale of the animals' pelts. She included horrifying photos of small animals with their legs caught in steel traps.

The Emergency Conservation Committee was the first truly grassroots environmental organization, and its main weapon was inflammatory pamphlets similar to Willard Van Name's "A Crisis in Conservation." Edge's scorching language belied her "high society" appearance and cultured voice. Someone who had attended one of her speeches once said to her, "Mrs. Edge, I never was so surprised as to see that you are a lady."

The pamphlets were having an effect. More than half of the Audubon Society's membership failed to renew. From a high of 8,400 in 1929, the membership in 1933 dropped to 3,400. Many of the members chose to join the Emergency Conservation Committee instead.

This loss of membership and the perseverance of Rosalie Edge and the ECC forced Gilbert Pearson to resign as president of the National Audubon Society on October 30, 1934. The Audubon board of directors recommended changes in some of its more controversial relationships, including the organization's connection to sport hunters and gun companies. Pearson's successor, John H. Baker, also stopped the trapping of animals in the Rainey Wildlife Sanctuary.

Having successfully initiated some reform of the National Audubon Society, Edge and the ECC took on another issue. In the autumn, hawks, eagles, peregrines, ospreys, and other birds of prey migrate south from Canada and the northeastern United States, gliding on the winds rebounding off the Appalachian Mountain ridges. One section of the Kittatinny Ridge in eastern Pennsylvania forms a bowl that offers a spectacular view of the migrating birds flying south. Each autumn, hunters gathered to shoot the hawks. Some believed the birds were a threat to poultry and other area wildfowl. Others shot them for sport. The hunters left the dead or wounded birds where they fell.

Much disturbed by the carnage, Edge commented, "Man hates any creature that kills and eats what he wishes to kill and eat. He does not take into account the millions of rodent and insect pests that hawks consume."

In 1934, Edge asked the National Audubon Society to purchase the land as a private sanctuary for birds of prey. When the society failed to act, Edge leased the approximately 1,400 acres herself. She hired a young ornithologist from Boston, Maurice Broun, and his wife, Irma, to be curators of the property. Broun had become a member of the ECC because, he said, "Here was this woman in New York City who was doing things in conservation—very militant, very strident, very abrasive, but she was doing things. Getting things done."

The Brouns posted the property with signs that warned against hunting and trespassing and guarded the trails, sometimes facing down hunters who would casually cradle rifles in their arms with the muzzles pointed right at them.

After a few years, the hunters accepted the new situation, and the Brouns instead spent their time leading groups of bird watchers or Girl Scouts or organizing the many volunteers who came each year to count the migrating birds. In 1938, Rosalie Edge bought the property outright and donated the land to the Hawk Mountain Sanctuary Association, an organization she founded and would lead for the rest of her life. Twenty-five years later, Rachel Carson would rely on the daily bird count at the sanctuary for research for her monumental book, *Silent Spring*.

Edge, however, did not confine her environmental concerns to birds or even to the eastern part of the United States. In 1937, when she was 60 years old, she confronted some angry loggers in Washington state who objected to her support of efforts to establish Olympic National Park. The 922,000-acre park was created in 1938.

Rosalie Edge (right) and a conservation colleague, Mrs. Raymond V. Ingersoll, protect one of the mature trees in Olympic National Park.

If burly loggers in the Northwest were unable to frighten her, neither could powerful governmental agencies. In 1934, she strongly criticized the U.S. Bureau of Biological Survey (BBS). At that time, the BBS was conducting a predator-control program, slaughtering wolves and coyotes and poisoning small animals because western ranchers did not like them. Edge referred to the BBS as the "Bureau of Destruction and Extermination" and tried to get the agency to end its predator-control program.

Edge made numerous visits to Capitol Hill to lobby Congress on behalf of laws such as those establishing Kings Canyon National Park in California. She convinced Interior Secretary Harold Ickes to support her campaign to add 6,000 acres of old-growth sugar pine forest to California's Yosemite National Park. Eventually, however, Edge would have doubts as to whether aligning herself with the government was a good idea. "I feel that we have perhaps moved too far from our old policy of arousing public interest first, and then enlisting the support of the government," she wrote to Irving Brant in 1941.

While Edge could be charming, her inflexibility and sometimes difficult personality alienated some, including other environmentalists. Even Irving Brant and Willard Van Name were not immune to her sharp tongue, and both eventually left the ECC. Edge did reconcile with her old adversary, however. Although she had withdrawn from an active role in the National Audubon Society, in autumn 1962 she decided to attend the organization's annual meeting in Corpus Christi, Texas.

When the Audubon officials heard that she was there, they did not know what to do. She had, after all, been responsible for the loss of almost half their membership 30 years earlier. But now she was a major figure in the conservation world. Should they acknowledge her presence or ignore her?

The organization's president, Carl W. Buchheister, made the final decision. "Rosalie Edge . . . is the officer of two national conservation organizations," he said. "We will ask her to sit on the dais as an honored guest." And she accepted the invitation.

At a reception before the banquet, Edge found herself the center of attention among other notables, including a U.S. senator and the governor of Texas. At the dinner that evening, the Audubon members rose to their feet and gave Edge a standing ovation when Buchheister introduced her.

After the convention, Edge returned to New York and told her son, Peter, "I have made peace with the National Audubon Society." Three weeks later, on November 30, 1962, at the age of 85, Rosalie Edge died. Without its vibrant leader, the Emergency Conservation Committee ceased to exist.

Hawks and other birds of prey still soar over Hawk Mountain Sanctuary during the late summer and autumn months, carefully counted and monitored by many volunteers. The sanctuary has increased in size to 2,380 acres. Its membership has soared. Nine thousand now belong to the association, and nature lovers from all over North America visit Hawk Mountain Sanctuary to experience the wild beauty of these birds who fly free through the efforts of Rosalie Edge.

Rand Aldo Leopold (1887-1948) challenged people to begin "thinking like a mountain." He wanted them to see the whole environment and to understand that they are part of the land, not masters of it.

4

Aldo Leopold
Green Fire

One day Aldo Leopold, a forester who believed in the right of human beings to control nature, shot a wolf and watched her die. Starting that day, his thinking about the interdependence between the land and the creatures and plants it supports began to change:

> We reached the old wolf in time to watch a fierce green fire dying in her eyes. . . . I realized then, and have known ever since, that there was something new to me in those eyes—something known only to her and to the mountain.

A wolf would force Aldo Leopold to rethink his beliefs about the value of predators and the role of humans in the natural world.

When Leopold saw the wolf die that day, a seed of doubt was planted in his mind about what he and the other foresters had done. It was a seed that would not bear fruit until many years later when Aldo Leopold began to question the right of human beings to dominate nature. Slowly, he would come to believe that nature was quite capable of managing itself. In his book, *A Sand County Almanac*, Leopold would later articulate what he called a land ethic—a belief that "changes the role of homo sapiens from conqueror of the land community to plain member and citizen of it." This book continues to serve as the "bible" of the American environmental movement.

Rand Aldo Leopold was born on January 11, 1887, in Burlington, Iowa, the first child of Carl and Clara Starker Leopold. He grew up in a large home overlooking the Mississippi River, along the migratory path of many ducks and geese. He spent much of his boyhood along the banks of the river and in the nearby marshes. There he hunted and fished and enjoyed all that the natural world offered. An inquisitive child, Aldo loved to study animals as much as he loved to hunt them. Later, when he was a student at Lawrenceville Preparatory School, his friends nicknamed him "the naturalist."

There was little doubt about Leopold's career path. In 1908, he graduated with a degree in science from Yale University. A year later, he earned a master's degree in forestry from Yale University and immediately joined the U.S. Forest Service. Forest assistant Leopold was stationed in the new Apache National Forest, in what was then the Arizona Territory. (Arizona would become the 48th state in 1912.)

The match between this new national forest and the young forester was a good one. It was also a good time to enter the field of forestry. Between 1901 and 1909, President Theodore Roosevelt had increased the national forest acreage from 46 to 148 million. This gave Leopold and his fellow foresters plenty of ground to cover.

Although the size of the forests had increased, the prevalent Forest Service philosophy was decidedly utilitarian: humans should use everything in the forests for their own benefit. The extermination of predators, such as mountain lions, wolves, and bears, was one management strategy that Leopold and his colleagues accepted without question. The government allowed the extermination because the predators competed with humans in hunting animals such as deer and elk.

Then one day on a survey expedition early in his career, Leopold and some other foresters shot a mother wolf and her cubs as they played together in the forest. He watched her die:

> I was young then, and full of trigger-itch; I thought that because fewer wolves meant more deer, that no wolves would mean hunters' paradise. But after seeing the green fire die, I sensed that neither the wolf nor the mountain agreed with such a view.

The government's extermination policy proved to be shortsighted. Lacking natural predators such as wolves to thin the herds, populations of deer and elk grew unchecked. Soon there was not enough food for all of them, and large numbers of the animals died of starvation or disease.

In 1911, the Forest Service transferred Leopold to the Carson National Forest, a million-acre forest in northern New Mexico Territory. He was promoted to supervisor there in 1912, the year New Mexico became a state. That October, he married Estella Bergere, a schoolteacher from a wealthy Santa Fe family. She would become his lifelong partner and supporter of his work and mother of their five children.

Forest Supervisor Harry C. Hall (right) had been appointed to restore the range in the Carson National Forest, which previous rangers had allowed to be grazed without limitation. He was assisted by deputy forest supervisor Aldo Leopold (left, astride his horse Polly). Forest Assistant Ira T. Yarnell poses in the center.

Leopold's career—and life—almost ended in 1913 when he became seriously ill with *nephritis*, a failure of the kidneys. During his 18-month recovery period, he had a great deal of time to read, to think, and to question. He frequently thought about the wildlife populations that had been vastly depleted because of sport hunting and loss of habitat. New homes and businesses often were built in areas that once had provided a *habitat*, or home, for wildlife species. The Leopolds' first child was born during this time, and Aldo Leopold worried that his son would never know the woods as he had. He began to consider wild game less as fodder for sport and more as an integral part of the whole forest ecosystem—as important as trees and soil and water. He began to realize that all species were connected and that the good health of one depended upon the good health of all the others.

By the time Leopold returned to work in October 1914, he had taken a giant step forward in his thinking. He had concluded that a healthy ecosystem requires planning. To ensure this, he said, the Forest Service must have a game-management program. Leopold argued that the government should not just protect grasslands for grazing and timber for logging. It should also preserve wildlife habitat to guarantee healthy animal populations.

After his illness, the Forest Service stationed Leopold in its southwest district office in Albuquerque, New Mexico. There he was in charge of recreation, publicity, and wildlife-protection issues. The job was perfect because it allowed him to organize game-management programs and work on behalf of wildlife protection. In 1915, he wrote the first guidebook for foresters, *Game and Fish Handbook*.

Leopold also branched out on his own, speaking to ranchers and local citizens' groups about the need for wildlife conservation. With other interested individuals,

74

he established the New Mexico Game Protective Association (NMGPA). This organization sought to reform the state game and fish administration, establish better wildlife law enforcement (in those days, very few arrests were made for breaches of wildlife laws), and create game refuges. Leopold served as writer, editor, designer, publisher, and circulation manager for *The Pine Cone*, the NMGPA's publication. A talented writer, Leopold's articles—most of which were about the need for stricter wildlife-protection regulations—were also being published in other journals on an increasingly frequent basis.

It was about this time that Leopold's campaign to protect certain wildlands through wilderness preservation began. In 1921, he and fellow forester Arthur Carhart successfully lobbied their superiors to preserve a beautiful undeveloped area in Colorado's White River National Forest. As Carhart and Leopold pointed out:

> There is a limit to the number of lakes in existence; there is a limit to the mountainous areas of the world, and in each one of these situations there are portions of natural scenic beauty which are God-made, and the beauties of which of a right should be the property of all people.

Leopold wrote an article for the *Journal of Forestry* in 1921 in which he defined wilderness as a "continuous stretch of country preserved in its natural state, open to lawful hunting and fishing, . . . and kept devoid of roads, artificial trails, cottages, or other works of man."

Leopold knew that if the United States was to preserve its precious heritage of wildlands for future generations, the government must act quickly. With encroaching development and other destructive activities, it might soon be too late to halt the devastation. "It will be much easier to keep wilderness areas than to create them," he wrote. He recommended that the government preserve one particular wilderness area: a half-million-acre parcel of land in New Mexico's Gila National Forest, an area isolated by mountains and canyons.

On June 3, 1924, the Forest Service declared 574,000 acres of the Gila National Forest as the first designated wilderness area in a national forest. This designation laid the groundwork for passage of the historic Wilderness Act 40 years later.

Five days before the Forest Service's action, Leopold had left New Mexico for Madison, Wisconsin, to become associate director of the U.S. Forest Products Laboratory, a research unit of the Forest Service. When a promised promotion to director never came, he resigned from the Forest Service in 1928.

Leopold then became game consultant for the Sporting Arms and Ammunitions Manufacturers Institute. One of his responsibilities was to direct a five-state survey of game—the first intensive study of the American game population ever undertaken. Leopold used some of the results from his surveys in his book, *Game Management*, which was published in 1933. Leopold said that he

The Gila Wilderness Area in southwestern New Mexico was preserved by the Forest Service in 1924 at the suggestion of Aldo Leopold. It was the first of many such areas. Today, the wilderness system protects 104 million acres of national forest, park, and refuge lands.

wanted the book "to interpret for the thinking sportsman or nature-lover the significance of some of the things he sees while afield with gun or glass or does in his capacity as a voting conservationist."

The book also helped Leopold's life take on a new dimension. The University of Wisconsin at Madison created a course in game management expressly so that Leopold could teach it. This action made him the first professor of game management in the country. When Leopold faced his first class of students in January 1934,

In his new role as a professor of game management, Aldo Leopold examines gray partridge specimens.

none of them knew that he had just been appointed by President Franklin Roosevelt to study the decline in duck populations. Two other prominent conservationists—Thomas Beck and Jay "Ding" Darling—served on what became known as the "Duck Committee."

Later that year, Leopold and other faculty members and students began work on the Arboretum, a 245-acre farm purchased by the university. They wanted to restore the land—which had been cleared, plowed, and drained like most of Wisconsin—to its original habitat with areas of pine and hardwood trees, marshes, grasses, and wildflowers. This was a timely and useful study because the drought of the 1930s was blowing away millions of bushels of topsoil due to poor farming practices.

In 1935, Leopold and his family began their own private arboretum when they bought an abandoned farm in Sauk County, Wisconsin. Leopold wanted to return the worn-out, sandy soil—which had once supported prairies and pine forests—to its natural state. Each weekend, the Leopold family would visit the farm and plant wildflowers and pine trees. One year, they planted as many as 6,000 trees. During these visits, Leopold jotted down his observations on nature—soil, trees, birds, and wildlife.

The same year he bought the farm, Leopold became one of the eight cofounders of The Wilderness Society. This organization dedicates itself to preserving wilderness and wildlife; to protecting America's prime forests, parks, rivers, deserts, and shorelines; and to fostering the idea

"The Shack" on the Leopolds' worn-out farm that the family labored to restore to its natural state. Leopold's wife, Estella, can be seen in the window, their daughter, Nina, is outside.

that land should be treated in a way that benefits the whole environment—wildlife, trees, soil, water—and not only people. Today, The Wilderness Society has approximately 250,000 members and has been at the forefront of every battle to save America's threatened wilderness areas.

During the 1940s, Aldo Leopold polished his notes and journal entries from his time at the family's farm and turned them into a book, *A Sand County Almanac.* For seven years, he tried to get his book published. Finally, on

April 14, 1948, an editor from Oxford University Press called to say the press would like to publish his book.

Seven days later, while working on his farm, Leopold spotted a fire on the next property. His youngest daughter, Estella, went to a neighbor's home to call the fire department. While his wife patrolled near Aldo's beloved pine trees to keep sparks from crossing the road to the Leopold farm, Leopold rushed to put out the fire. Other neighbors joined the fight.

When the fire was extinguished (without any damage to the Leopolds' land), they found Aldo Leopold lying dead in the grass. The 61-year-old Leopold had suffered a heart attack and died while fighting to save the land.

A Sand County Almanac was published the following year. With its theme of commitment and obligation to the land, it is considered to be the most important book of the conservation movement. The *Almanac* includes Leopold's thoughtful essays on the interdependence of all life and the need to adopt a land ethic. In this classic volume, Leopold defined this revolutionary ethic:

> All ethics so far evolved rest upon a single premise: that the individual is a member of a community of interdependent parts. His instincts prompt him to compete for his place in that community, but his ethics prompt him also to cooperate. . . . The land ethic simply enlarges the boundaries of the community to include soils, waters, plants, and animals, or collectively: the land.

Olaus Murie (1889-1963) and his wife, Margaret (b. 1902), worked together to preserve the natural habitats—and predators—of elk, caribou, and other animals they had spent years studying in the field.

5

Olaus and Margaret Murie
Wilderness Protectors

*W*hile growing up, Olaus Murie and his brother, Adolph, often hunted and fished in a forested area along the Red River that flows between Minnesota and North Dakota. The boys called the area "The Wilderness," not knowing that both would choose field biology as their profession and spend much of their adult lives in wild places. Olaus would also become a prominent leader in the movement to protect American wilderness.

Born in Moorhead, Minnesota, on March 1, 1889, Olaus Johan Murie was the son of Norwegian immigrants

Joachim D. and Marie Frimanslund Murie. He was only 10 when his father died, leaving his wife and three sons very little money.

Olaus earned extra income for his family by delivering pails of milk before and after school. For his work on area vegetable farms he was paid in vegetables. He also hunted small game for the family to eat. Although he lacked material possessions, Olaus grew up in a close and loving family amid natural surroundings that any child would have envied. In his later life, he looked back on his youth fully satisfied with the wonderful "open air farm life we led."

Murie won a scholarship to Fargo College across the Red River in North Dakota, where he became the protégé of biology professor Arthur M. Bean. When Bean accepted a new position at Pacific University in Oregon, he took Murie along as his assistant. After receiving a B.A. from Pacific in 1912, Murie worked for the Oregon State Game Commission, collecting wildlife specimens and photographing wildlife.

In 1914, the Carnegie Museum of Natural History in Pittsburgh hired Murie to accompany an expedition to the Hudson Bay in subarctic Canada to collect bird specimens. Murie fell in love with the area, and he decided to stay when the expedition ended. "The north had appealed to me—its freedom and its beauty," he later wrote in his book, *Journey to the Far North*. "I did not have definite plans, but I just wanted to be there."

Murie spent much of 1915 accompanying Eskimos (also known as Inuits) and Cree Indians on their hunts. Throughout his stay in Canada, he took scientific notes and prepared bird specimens, which he hoped to sell to the Carnegie Museum when he returned to the United States.

The Carnegie Museum hired Murie once again in 1917, this time to join the first scientific expedition to trek across Labrador in eastern Canada. The team of three men hired five American Indians to help them paddle 750 miles north from Clarke City on the St. Lawrence River to Fort Chimo, a trading post on Hudson Strait. They often got lost because of inaccurate maps. The region was so desolate that between May and mid-August, the team encountered only three other people.

By 1920, Murie's reputation as a field biologist and as someone who could communicate with the Inuits had grown. For these reasons, the U.S. Bureau of Biological Survey (now the U.S. Fish and Wildlife Service) invited him to head a scientific expedition to Alaska to study its wildlife—particularly the habits and migrations of wild caribou herds. At the time, Alaska was not a state. The United States had purchased the territory from Russia in 1867, and most of Alaska's ecology remained a mystery.

Murie immersed himself completely in the project, which took nearly six years to finish. He traveled by boat or on foot during the summer and by dogsled or on snow-shoes in the winter. Murie visited all the principal caribou

Caribou live in arctic and subarctic regions and have sharp hoofs that enable them to dig through the snow and ice to find grass and lichens to eat.

ranges and interviewed everyone—hunters, Eskimos, and travelers—who might possibly add to his knowledge.

Dogsledding held a particular fascination for Murie, and was his favorite form of transportation during his field work. His dogs were the subject of several articles. In one recollection of the Alaska Range, he wrote:

The dogs were eager to be up and doing, to go somewhere, to pull the sled. I had a similar feeling, wanting to clamber over the mountains, to discover, to achieve. I suppose we can say that both man and dog have the joyous impulse to *do*.

Murie's findings about the caribou were published in 1935. In his report, he challenged the commonly held belief that wolves and sport hunting were the primary cause of the decline of the caribou population. "The caribou's greatest menace is not the wolf, nor the hunter," he wrote, "but man's economic development, principally the raising of reindeer." The U.S. government had introduced reindeer to the area, hoping the Eskimos would benefit economically from the animal. But the reindeer competed with the native caribou for food, and their introduction failed to help the Eskimos either.

In 1924, Murie set out on a different kind of expedition: marriage. He had met his future bride, Margaret "Mardy" Thomas, in 1921 when he was visiting friends in Fairbanks, Alaska, and she was home on summer vacation. Most of their courtship was conducted by mail.

Mardy had lived in Alaska since she was nine. She attended colleges in Oregon and Boston before entering the new University of Alaska, where she became the first woman graduate. After college, Mardy traveled with her mother to Anvik, on the shores of the Yukon River. There, in a small log church, she and Olaus Murie were married on August 19, 1924. The wedding was set to be held on Mardy's 22nd birthday, August 18, but she had arrived late. Some thought the marriage would not work because of Olaus's strenuous lifestyle, but Mardy loved both the wilderness and her husband.

When Olaus put his bride to work on their honeymoon labeling mammal specimens, mostly mice, she did so without complaint. The Muries would be true partners

Mardy Murie looks at Lobo Lake in Alaska from their base camp. Although this photo was taken in the 1950s, it illustrates how the Muries typically lived while working in the field.

in both their professional and private lives. During their marriage, Mardy worked at her husband's side on all but one of his expeditions. When negotiating the terms for these expeditions, Olaus Murie told the organizers that he wanted to take along his family—which later included their three children—and the organizers always let him. "I suppose they knew they would have to allow it, or fire him!" observed Mardy Murie.

The President's Committee on Outdoor Recreation appointed a special elk commission in 1927 to investigate why large numbers of North American elk were disappearing from their original ranges. The commission turned the task over to the Bureau of Biological Survey (BBS), and the BBS hired Olaus Murie. His mission was to conduct a comprehensive study of the Wyoming elk population. With some 20,000 animals, this was the largest elk herd in the world.

Olaus and Mardy reluctantly left their beloved Alaska and settled in Moose, Wyoming, near the Teton Mountains. As was the case with all of his studies, Olaus Murie became totally absorbed in his subject. He meticulously analyzed elk habitat, migrating patterns, physiology, predators, and food habits. He followed the elk from birth to death and developed an affection for them, recalling:

> After a winter of living with the wapiti [an American Indian name for elk] through their dark days, watching them die, examining them, working in snow and blizzard

and below-zero cold, trudging home across the fields night after night with cold and bloody hands and a few more unpleasant data in my notebook—you can imagine my joy at the spring release of the survivors out onto the greening hillsides, up through the aspen groves, and on north to first verdure and new smooth red-brown coats and the endless freedom of the summer world.

Murie concluded that one of the reasons elk numbers were declining was that the U.S. government as well as trappers, ranchers, farmers, and sport hunters were killing the area's natural predators—wolves, bears, and coyotes. Without predators to keep them out, animals not native to the area, such as deer, cattle, and sheep, competed with the elk for food. Forced out of their natural habitat by the competition, the elk had to feed on coarse forage that tore open the skin of their mouths, resulting in fatal infections.

After years of studying wildlife, Murie began to question the government policy that assumed all predators were undesirable. Instead, he came to believe that all wildlife had an intrinsic value of its own and should be protected. Murie also disagreed with the prevailing notion that people had the right to use public lands for their own benefit regardless of the consequences. At the time, people used public lands in every way they could think of to enrich themselves—they dammed wild rivers, logged ancient forests, and overgrazed grasslands with too much livestock.

Murie saw the harm such abuse had caused and concluded that for an ecosystem to remain healthy, it had to be left alone. He arrived at these conclusions while still working for the government, and he made no secret of his newfound beliefs. Historian Donald Worster described Murie at the time as a "tolerated but unheeded maverick," adding, "It could not have been easy for such a peaceable man to be on the outs with so many of his colleagues for so long." Olaus Murie persisted more than two decades in his efforts to change the bureau's policy regarding the necessity of predators to the balance of nature.

The BBS was not easily converted, however. At a 1937 wildlife conference, the agency refused to allow Murie to speak in favor of coyotes. Eight years later, the Fish and Wildlife Service, successor to the Bureau of Biological Survey, would not publish Olaus Murie's study of coyotes because it criticized the government's predator-extermination policy.

In 1945, Murie retired from government service and became part-time director of The Wilderness Society, the group he had helped to found in 1935. He refused to move to Washington, D.C., where the society was located, so the group allowed him to work from his Moose, Wyoming, home. There, the Muries greeted a steady stream of admirers who visited their home, eager to learn what they could from such esteemed conservationists.

After World War II ended in 1945, developers all across the United States began to clear large tracts of

This photograph of Mardy and Olaus Murie was taken at the annual meeting of The Wilderness Society held in Montana in 1953.

land to construct homes and businesses. If someone did not act soon, the Muries believed, the wilderness would be lost. So Murie wrote articles, lectured, and testified at hearings. "We had become immersed in the conservation battle," Mardy remembered, "and we both knew that life was blooming, expanding, growing because of the new work Olaus had undertaken."

In the summer of 1956, Olaus and Mardy Murie led an expedition into Alaska's Brooks Range. There they hoped to gather the scientific evidence necessary to have the northeastern corner of the area designated a national wildlife range, which would protect it from development. They observed, photographed, tracked, and took notes on everything they encountered along the way—from the smallest plants to the tallest trees, from the Arctic squirrel to the majestic caribou. After submitting their evidence to Congress, the Muries continued to actively promote the Arctic National Wildlife Range.

The right people listened to the Muries, and on December 7, 1960, Secretary of the Interior Fred A. Seaton signed an order creating the Arctic National Wildlife Range, a 9-million-acre preserve. The region, now called the Arctic National Wildlife Refuge, has been enlarged to 19 million acres.

During the late 1950s and early 1960s, Olaus Murie focused his energies on the passage of the Wilderness Act, which would make preservation of wilderness areas an official national policy. Mardy Murie said of his work, "That was an eight-year struggle."

Unfortunately, Olaus Murie did not live to see the fruits of his labors on behalf of the American wilderness. President Lyndon Johnson signed the historic Wilderness Act into law on September 3, 1964, almost a year after Murie's death on October 21, 1963. The Wilderness Act of 1964 protected 9 million acres of national forest wilderness lands from all development and other destructive human intrusions. Today, the National Wilderness

Preservation System encompasses approximately 104 million acres of land in national forests, national parks, and national wildlife refuges throughout the United States.

Margaret Murie was present at the signing, however, and she continued working on behalf of wilderness preservation long after Olaus's death. For a time, she worked out of the Seattle office of The Wilderness Society, giving lectures and testifying at congressional hearings. She also wrote two books, *Two in the Far North* (1962); *Island Between*, a novel (1978); and coauthored *Wapiti Wilderness* (1966) with her husband.

Like Olaus, Mardy Murie received a number of awards for her work on behalf of the environment, including the National Audubon Medal in 1980 (the Audubon Medal had been awarded to Olaus 21 years earlier); and, in 1983, the Sierra Club's highest honor, the John Muir Award, for outstanding service on behalf of the environment. (Mardy was the first woman to ever receive this award. Olaus Murie had received the John Muir Award in 1963.) They were both also honored with the Aldo Leopold Memorial Medal. More recently, in January 1998, Mardy received the Presidential Medal of Freedom from President Bill Clinton. The medal is the highest civilian honor that the nation can bestow.

Following Olaus's death, Mardy Murie continued to live in their log home in Moose, Wyoming, where for so many years she and Olaus had shared their lives and their work on behalf of the environment.

The Muries outside their log home in Moose,
Wyoming, in 1961. During the winter, when roads
to their home were snowbound, they would ski to their
car, which they left parked by a main highway. From
there, they would drive to town for supplies.

A scientist who wrote eloquently about the natural world, Rachel Carson (1907-1964) stirred many people to action with her book, Silent Spring, *which detailed the dangers of pesticides.*

6

Rachel Carson
Breaking the Silence

*I*n her 1962 book, *Silent Spring*, Rachel Carson sounded a warning about the chemicals that were being used all around us:

> These sprays, dusts, and aerosols are now applied almost universally to farms, gardens, forests, and homes—non-selective chemicals that have the power to kill every insect, the "good" and the "bad," to still the song of birds and the leaping of fish in the streams, to coat the leaves with a deadly film, and to linger on in the soil—all this though the intended target may be only a few weeds or insects.

Her publication alerted the public to the uncontrolled use of *pesticides*—chemicals that kill insect pests. While these chemicals were poisoning the environment, the government and the industries assured the public that pesticides and *herbicides* (weed killers) were not only safe, but beneficial. Disease-carrying insects could be wiped out and crop yields increased.

Carson, however, wanted people to weigh the evidence she had accumulated against the assurances of the government and the producers of these chemicals. She knew there was cause for concern. That is why she wrote the book that Supreme Court Justice William O. Douglas would call "the most important chronicle of this century for the human race."

Rachel Louise Carson was born in Springdale, Pennsylvania, on May 27, 1907. Her parents, Robert Warden Carson and Maria Frazier McLean Carson, encouraged their three children to learn about birds and flowers and all aspects of their natural surroundings. "I can remember no time when I wasn't interested in the out-of-doors and the whole world of nature," Carson later recalled. Maria Carson also nurtured Rachel's interest in reading and writing. When she was only 10 years old, Rachel had her first story published in *St. Nicholas*, a children's magazine.

Intending to become a writer, Carson entered the Pennsylvania College for Women (now Chatham College) in 1925. When she took a required course in

Rachel Carson (left) with her older siblings Robert, shown here in his World War I uniform in 1917 or 1918, and Marian

biology during her sophomore year, the subject so fascinated her that she decided to become a scientist instead. At the time, some of her college counselors tried to dissuade Carson from embarking on a career in science, believing that such work was more appropriate for a man.

Today, Carson's choice between becoming a writer or a scientist would not be as difficult. "I thought I had to be one or the other," she later wrote. "It never occurred to me, or apparently to anyone else, that I could combine two careers." Carson graduated from college *magna cum laude* in 1929.

Ever since she had been a child, the sea had always fascinated Carson. But she did not actually see the ocean until she was 21 and worked at Woods Hole Marine Biological Laboratory on the Atlantic Ocean during the summer. Here she spent many hours studying tissue samples of marine animals under a microscope as well as time along the ocean front. This experience convinced her to specialize in marine biology and laid the foundation for her future books about the sea.

She received a master's degree in zoology from Johns Hopkins University in Baltimore in 1932, and then taught part-time there and at the University of Maryland. Her parents had moved to Baltimore while she was a student there, so they all lived together during the financially difficult years of the Great Depression. Then, in 1935, both her father and her sister, Marian, died. Marian's two young daughters were left in the care of Carson and her mother, and Carson realized she needed a full-time job to support them.

In 1936, Rachel Carson took the civil service test for the position of junior aquatic biologist with the U.S. Bureau of Fisheries. She received the top score. Carson became only the second woman ever to work at the agency in a nonclerical position.

Although the agency hired her as a biologist, Carson's job entailed a great deal of writing. She wrote a series of conservation pamphlets and radio scripts about the bureau. In her second year with the bureau, Carson's supervisor asked her to write an introduction to those radio broadcasts. They had been well received and were now being published in a government booklet. The result was "too literary" for her supervisor's purposes, but he liked the piece and advised Carson to send it to the *Atlantic Monthly*, which she did.

Much to Rachel Carson's astonishment, the *Atlantic* accepted the essay—"Undersea"—and published it in September 1937. The essay caught the attention of Quincy Howe, an editor with Simon and Schuster, a New York publisher. Howe asked Carson if she would consider expanding her essay into a book about the ocean.

The book, *Under the Sea-Wind*, was, in Carson's words, "a series of descriptive narratives unfolding successively the life of the shore, the open sea, and the sea bottom." She took great pains to write so that she would be understood by readers with no scientific background. Unfortunately, Simon and Schuster published *Under the Sea-Wind* in November 1941, just before the United States entered World War II. This was not a good time to sell books. While *Under the Sea-Wind* was not a bestseller, both the scientific and the literary communities praised it.

Rachel Carson enjoyed the field research she conducted while a biologist with the U.S. Fish and Wildlife Service. Here she and colleague Robert W. Hines collect specimens of tide life in Ohio Key, Florida.

In 1940, the Bureau of Fisheries merged with the U.S. Bureau of Biological Survey to become the U.S. Fish and Wildlife Service (FWS). In 1946, Carson became an information specialist, and from 1949 until her retirement, her title was biologist and chief editor.

In 1951, Carson's second book, *The Sea Around Us*, was published. She again won praise from scientific and literary scholars, but this time sales were brisk. *The Sea Around Us* stayed on the bestseller list for 86 weeks. The book was popular because, as one reviewer noted, Carson had the ability to "fuse poetry and science into that rare commodity known as literature."

The success of *The Sea Around Us* enabled Carson to resign from her government job in 1952 and concentrate on her writing full time. She now had enough money to build a cottage on land overlooking Sheepscot Bay in West Southport, Maine. Carson treasured this beautiful spot on the ocean with a view of the rocky shoreline.

Carson spent all of her summers at the cottage. Much of the time, she was up to her knees in the tide pools, examining sea life along the coast of Maine. The research she did at the cottage became the basis for her third book, *The Edge of the Sea*, which was published in 1955. It, too, became a bestseller. Carson's first three books had brought her fame and a moderate fortune, but her next and most important book would have an impact that she hardly could have imagined.

Since the 1940s, companies had been producing a new chemical called dichloro-diphenyl-trichloro-ethane. Commonly known as DDT, the chemical killed lice on people and controlled other insect pests. Although the public knew little about this pesticide, the scientific community was becoming aware of the potentially damaging side effects of DDT. In 1944, the American Association of Economic Entomologists published a paper to correct "misunderstanding, overoptimism, and distorted impressions" about the value of the new chemical:

> DDT will not kill all important insect pests. It will kill many beneficial insects which are allies of mankind against the destructive species. Because of its toxicity to a wide variety of insects, its large-scale use might create problems which do not now exist.

By 1955, approximately 600 million pounds of DDT had been sprayed on crops all across the United States. In 1958, Olga Owens Huckins, a former newspaper writer and a friend of Carson's, wrote a letter to the *Boston Herald* criticizing the state's mosquito-control program:

> The "harmless" shower bath [of DDT] killed seven of our lovely songbirds outright. We picked up three dead bodies the next morning right by the door. . . . The next day three were scattered around the bird bath. (I had emptied it and scrubbed it after the spraying but YOU CAN NEVER KILL DDT.) On the following day one robin dropped suddenly from a branch in our woods. We were too heartsick to hunt for other corpses. All of these birds died horribly, and in the same way. Their bills were gaping open, and their splayed claws were drawn up to their breasts in agony.

Huckins sent a copy of her letter to Carson, hoping that her friend would use her influence to persuade the state of Massachusetts to end its spraying program.

During the 1950s, specially equipped planes such as this one sprayed millions of pounds of DDT over farm crops, marshes, and even private homes in an effort to control insects that damaged produce or were considered to be a nuisance.

Carson responded to this cry for help. Her research revealed that more and more baby birds either never hatched or were born grossly malformed. Other fertilized eggs were not developing into chicks at all. Many birds had become sterile. Bird populations were decreasing, and all scientific evidence pointed to DDT as the cause.

"The more I learned about the use of pesticides, the more appalled I became," Carson later recalled. "I realized that here was the material for a book." That book was *Silent Spring*. As Carson wrote to Paul Brooks, her editor at Houghton Mifflin:

> I shall be able to support a claim to even more serious and insidious effects, which include the most basic functions of every living cell. . . . I shall be able to show that the chemicals used as insecticides interfere with many of the enzymes that control the most basic functions of the body.

In addition to their dangers, according to Carson, spraying operations were ultimately self-defeating because insects very quickly become resistant to insecticides. Consequently, she said, those who use the pesticides kill wildlife and contaminate foods in vain. The insects, in contrast, would adapt and survive.

Knowing that *Silent Spring* had to be based on the soundest scientific evidence, Carson set to work accumulating facts from every possible source—congressional testimony; experts in the medical, agricultural, and other professional fields; independent scientists knowledgeable about pesticides; and, of course, her own immense store of knowledge.

She also monitored a 1957 court case in which residents of Long Island, New York, lost their suit to prevent the state from spraying DDT to control gypsy moths. Carson described the program in *Silent Spring*:

They sprayed truck gardens and dairy farms, fish ponds and salt marshes. They sprayed the quarter-acre lots of suburbia, drenching a housewife making a desperate effort to cover her garden before the roaring plane reached her, and showering insecticide over children at play and commuters at railway stations.

The four years Rachel Carson labored over *Silent Spring* were difficult ones. Her mother died; she adopted her grandnephew, who had been orphaned at age 5; and she underwent treatments for breast cancer. But in 1962, Carson finished her manuscript and sent it to William Shawn, editor of the *New Yorker* magazine, for his reaction. He responded so enthusiastically that Carson said, "I knew my message would get across."

Shawn serialized *Silent Spring* in the *New Yorker* beginning on June 16, 1962, and Carson became the center of a national controversy that made for a "noisy summer," as the newspaper headlines proclaimed. The chemical and agricultural industries immediately attacked her credentials as a scientist and attempted to demean her as a person—labeling her nothing more than a "bird-lover." They also spent enormous sums of money to convince the public that no cause for alarm existed.

In spite of the publicity to discredit Carson and her work, the book sold widely when it was published in September. *Silent Spring* reached the bestseller list in just a few weeks, and many scientists confirmed the accuracy of her research. Carson did not often respond to critics,

The success of The Sea Around Us *changed Rachel Carson's life, allowing her to become a full-time writer. Her later book,* Silent Spring, *in turn, changed the way many people thought about the environment. Vice-President Al Gore, who was influenced by Carson's work, wrote an introduction to this 1994 edition.*

preferring to let her work speak for itself. But she explained her position this way:

> It would not be possible to abandon all chemicals tomorrow even if we wanted to. What we can and must do is to begin a determined and purposeful program of substitution, of replacing dangerous chemicals with new and even more efficient methods as rapidly as we can.

In October 1962, four months after *Silent Spring* first appeared in the *New Yorker*, President John F. Kennedy, who personally admired Carson's work, established the President's Science Advisory Committee. The purpose of the committee was to investigate the dangers and benefits of pesticide use. In May 1963, the committee issued its report, recommending that "elimination of the use of persistent toxic pesticides should be the goal." *Science*, the journal of the American Association for the Advancement of Science, commented that the committee's findings added "up to a fairly thorough-going vindication of Rachel Carson's *Silent Spring* thesis."

In reaction to *Silent Spring*, by the end of 1962, state legislatures across the country had introduced 40 bills regulating the use of pesticides. *Silent Spring* was translated into a dozen languages, including Swedish, French, German, Italian, and Japanese. As a result, Sweden and several other countries passed laws regulating pesticide use. Yet, largely because of the opposition of the chemical industry, it took the U.S. government 10 years to enact similar legislation. Finally, in 1972, after much

Rachel Carson counting migratory birds atop Hawk Mountain in Pennsylvania, the sanctuary founded by Rosalie Edge in 1934

study and debate, the Environmental Protection Agency (EPA) banned the use of DDT. (The EPA, established in 1970, had been Carson's idea. She believed that environmental issues should be under the jurisdiction of one bureau rather than scattered among many different departments.) Four years later, Congress passed the Toxic Substances Control Act, banning or strictly controlling the use of many other pesticides and toxic chemicals.

Despite her cancer, Carson spent the two years after the publication of *Silent Spring* spreading the word about the dangers of pesticides. She testified before Congress and accepted many speaking invitations before her illness forced her to stop working. Rachel Carson died of cancer on April 14, 1964, at the age of 56.

Before she died, Rachel Carson received numerous honors, including the Conservationist of the Year Award from the National Wildlife Federation in 1963. She was also the first woman to receive the National Audubon Society Medal. Upon accepting the award, she warned, "Conservation is a cause that has no end. There is no point at which we will say 'our work is finished.'" In 1969, five years after her death, the Department of the Interior bestowed on Carson an honor that would have pleased her: the government changed the name of the Coastal Maine Refuge to the Rachel Carson National Wildlife Refuge.

As head of the Sierra Club and founder of Earth Island Institute, David Brower roused ordinary people to play a role in protecting the environment.

112

7

David Brower
Letting Rivers Run

*D*avid Brower had grown up a rather shy and quiet child who would have done anything to avoid speaking in public. But one summer, on a one-month wilderness outing with the Sierra Club, he was asked to talk about his feelings for the environment. The group was large— about 200 people. Speaking in front of so many people would usually have intimidated the young man.

Somehow Brower found himself talking easily and eloquently to a spellbound audience. He could never explain what happened that night around the campfire other than to say he felt something awaken in him. But for whatever reason, David Brower had found his niche. His newfound ability to inspire others through his public speaking would become his most powerful tool as an environmental leader and would spur many an audience into action.

David Ross Brower was born on July 1, 1912, in Berkeley, California, the third of four children of Ross and Mary Grace Barlow Brower. Growing up amid the natural beauty of northern California may have given birth to David's love of nature. When he was still a young boy, however, he learned to see nature in a whole new way.

David's mother went blind as the result of an inoperable brain tumor when he was eight years old. Because she loved the hills around their home, young David would take her on walks in the hills above Berkeley and describe in detail what he saw. In effect, he became his mother's eyes. "Looking for someone else may have sharpened my appreciation of the beauty in natural things," he said later.

In trying to observe as much as he could for his mother, David developed a keen eye for identifying flowers and animals. Butterflies became his specialty and, at age 15, he found one that had never been identified. The scientific Latin name for this butterfly subsequently honored its discoverer: *Anthocaris sara reakirtii broweri.*

Brower became a college student at the University of California at Berkeley, in 1929. But like many other students during the Great Depression, he had to drop out of school in 1931 for financial reasons. Not certain what he wanted to do with his life, he took a job as a clerk in a candy factory. In his free time, he became an enthusiastic hiker and mountain climber, overcoming a fear of heights that had plagued him since childhood.

In 1933, Brower took a seven-week backpacking trip in California's High Sierra with a friend, George Rockwood. That expedition would change his life. It was his first encounter with members of the Sierra Club, people who shared his love of the outdoors. John Muir, the first of the modern-day environmentalists, had founded the Sierra Club in 1892, asking its members to "explore, enjoy, and preserve" the mountains.

That same year, Brower met Ansel Adams, a renowned photographer of Yosemite and an active Sierra Club member. Adams would become a lifelong friend. Another friend, Dick Leonard, sponsored Brower as a member of the Sierra Club. (At the time, prospective members had to be recommended by someone who already was a member. Today, anyone who wishes to can become a member without having a sponsor.)

Brower had continued to work at the candy factory intermittently. But one day in 1935, he returned late for work from a climbing expedition in Canada to find that his job had been eliminated.

Losing his job did not concern Brower because he had already decided to focus his life on the outdoors and

David Brower leading the first ascent of Ship Rock in 1939. Located in the northwest corner of New Mexico, Ship Rock was considered the most difficult climb in the United States at the time.

the environment. With this in mind, he took a job as an office worker at Yosemite National Park in California, where he eventually became the publicity manager. On his days off, Brower climbed mountains, scaling 33 different peaks.

In 1941, Brower landed a job as an editor at the University of California Press. There he met Anne Hus, a fellow editor. That December, the United States entered World War II, and Brower joined the U.S. Army in 1942, serving with the U.S. Mountain Troops. Stationed in Colorado and West Virginia, he taught climbing techniques to the soldiers. Now a lieutenant, he married Anne Hus in 1943. He served as an intelligence officer in combat in the mountains of Italy and was awarded the Bronze Star.

When the war ended in 1945, David Brower returned home to his wife and the first of their four children and to his old job at the University of California Press. He became more involved with the Sierra Club, editing the *Sierra Club Bulletin* (now *Sierra* magazine) and following conservation issues in his spare time. The Alps he had climbed while in Italy, "the shattered remains of what must have been beautiful wildernesses," had saddened him. He did not want the Sierra Nevada Mountains to lose their wildness, and he worked harder than ever to save the region from the fate of the Alps.

In 1952, Brower's efforts on behalf of the Sierra Club were recognized when he was appointed the group's first full-time paid executive director. The Sierra Club had been an activist organization since John Muir's day. It engaged in battles with the government and commercial interests, such as its losing effort to save Yosemite's Hetch Hetchy Valley in the early part of the century. Following Muir's death in 1914, the club had concentrated its activism on issues concerning the Sierra Nevada.

When the board appointed Brower as executive director, it recommended that he use "friendly persuasion" when confronted with a controversial issue. But Brower had his own ideas. He wanted the organization to move in a new, more aggressive direction and to attract members who would be more action-oriented. He also wanted the organization to expand its horizons—to recruit members from across the United States so that the Sierra Club would become a truly national organization.

Brower's first battle as executive director involved the construction of two dams on the Green River in Dinosaur National Monument located on the Utah and Colorado border. The Interior Department's Bureau of Reclamation wanted to build the dams—called Echo Park and Split Mountain—as part of the billion-dollar Colorado River Storage Project that would provide water and power for the growing population in the western states. Environmentalists opposed the dams because they would violate the National Park Organic Act of 1916 (also known as the National Park Service Act). That piece of legislation stated that the purpose of national parks and monuments was "to conserve the scenery and the natural and historic objects and wildlife therein and to provide for the enjoyment of the same in such manner and by such means as will leave them unimpaired for the enjoyment of future generations."

Building dams in Dinosaur National Monument, which would flood the wild, isolated canyons, was a clear violation of the act. To surmount that obstacle, proponents of the dams had to obtain special permission from Congress to build them.

With the lines of battle drawn, David Brower set to work. In the summer of 1953, he arranged float trips through the rivers of the monument for journalists, politicians, and others interested in the area. "I have never had a scenic experience to equal that one," he said later. Brower traveled throughout the country and made speeches to educate the public about what the dams would do to their monument, reminding his audiences that all public lands belong to the American people.

Believing in the use of publicity to convey their message, Brower arranged for the publication of a book titled *This Is Dinosaur.* The book contained striking photographs of the beautiful river canyon in Dinosaur Valley, to show what would be lost if the valley was flooded. He testified before Congress against the dams, making sure every member received a copy of *This Is Dinosaur.* He showed the senators and representatives photos of Hetch Hetchy Valley before it was dammed in 1913. It had

David Brower often photographed or filmed the places he worked to preserve, using these visual records to persuade others to support his causes.

been a valley full of beautiful vegetation; afterwards, it was simply a pool of water surrounded by a muddy shoreline. He also made a film, *Two Yosemites*. "If we heed the lesson learned from the tragedy of the misplaced dam in Hetch Hetchy," Brower testified, "we can prevent a far more disastrous stumble in Dinosaur National Monument."

Brower and his colleagues even double-checked the Bureau of Reclamation's engineering analysis and found an error. The bureau had overestimated the water-saving superiority of the Dinosaur dams over other possible sites.

The perseverance and aggressive lobbying of David Brower and the Sierra Club paid off. In 1955, Congress eliminated the provision in the Colorado River project bill that would have allowed the two dams to be built in Dinosaur National Monument. Brower celebrated the victory with mixed emotions, however, because in exchange for canceling Echo Park and Split Mountain Dams, the Sierra Club directors agreed not to fight construction of Glen Canyon Dam in Utah. Brower failed to oppose this compromise even though he had never visited the canyon. It was a decision he would always regret. "I did not do what a leader should have done," he wrote in his book *Let the Mountains Talk, Let the Rivers Run,* "which was hop the next plane to the West Coast and rally the board to righteousness. Instead, I sat on my duff. . . . Now I have to live with that, the flooding of the place no one knew, Glen Canyon."

In 1963, as the construction of Glen Canyon Dam began to inundate one of the country's beautiful wild places, the Sierra Club took on another major campaign in which Brower again used publicity to appeal for help from the public. The Bureau of Reclamation wanted to build two dams in the Grand Canyon in Arizona. The dams would be popular, the bureau argued, because they would allow visitors to come closer to the canyon walls. In response, Brower prepared an advertisement asking the question: "Should We Also Flood the Sistine Chapel So Tourists Can Get Nearer the Ceiling?" Brower also placed full-page ads in the *New York Times* and the *Washington Post* that read: "This time it's the Grand Canyon they want to flood. The Grand Canyon."

The Colorado River cut this huge gorge called the Grand Canyon. The most scenic portion of the 200-mile long canyon is located in Arizona's Grand Canyon National Park, designated in 1919 and expanded in 1975.

Brower's ads succeeded in prompting many people to contact their congressional representatives. Congress voted against the dams, but Brower and the Sierra Club paid a price for their success. During the intense Grand Canyon campaign, the Internal Revenue Service determined that the organization had engaged in "substantial" political lobbying and revoked its prior tax-deductible status. The ruling could have inflicted a financial blow because donors were no longer allowed to deduct their contributions to the Sierra Club from their taxable income. One year later, however, the Sierra Club had gained more than 10,000 new members.

During the 1960s, Brower created a publishing program called the exhibit-format series as a way to educate and excite the public about America's wildlands. These 30 coffee-table books featured beautiful landscape photography and informative text. The first book, *This Is The American Earth*, released in 1960, included black-and-white photographs by Ansel Adams. Color photographs that brought the American wilderness into the homes of average citizens were used in later books. Without actually visiting the areas, people could see the magnificent lands that would be lost without government protection.

The publications spurred individuals to call or write their representatives in Congress, asking that various threatened areas be saved. That response was exactly what Brower had in mind. In 1964, the series received the Carey Thomas Award for excellence in book publishing.

As executive director of the Sierra Club in the 1950s and 1960s, Brower played a major role in the creation of four national parks: Kings Canyon and Redwood, both located in California, the North Cascades in Washington, and the Great Basin in Nevada. He also led efforts to enlarge the Arctic National Wildlife Refuge in Alaska and to create national seashores at Point Reyes in California, Cape Cod in Massachusetts, and Fire Island in New York.

Caribou graze near the peaks of Brooks Range, one of the northernmost mountain ranges in the world, in Alaska's Arctic National Wildlife Refuge. The refuge was established in 1960.

With his advertisements, books, and speeches, David Brower roused people to play a role in protecting the nation's natural heritage. In addition, he sent out "action alerts" to Sierra Club members, outlining current problems and then suggesting ways members could help.

In 1958, Brower initiated the Outdoor Recreation Resources Review Commission to study present and future recreation needs for all federal land systems. A direct result of that commission was the Land and Water Conservation Fund Act of 1964. This legislation provided funds for the federal acquisition and development of lands for national parks, wildlife refuges, wild and scenic rivers, and other federal conservation programs.

By the mid 1960s, the Sierra Club was regarded as the most influential environmental organization in the country. And it was Brower, said the *New York Times*, who had transformed the Sierra Club into "the gangbusters of the conservation movement." *Newsweek* called Brower "the club's slow-burning but incandescent firebrand," and *Life* magazine said that he was "his country's number one working conservationist."

While the world was praising David Brower, the Sierra Club's board of directors was trying to rein him in a bit. Although Brower's tactics were often successful, they were also expensive. The Sierra Club's beautiful coffee-table books, for example, were enormously costly to produce. Members of the board of directors began criticizing what they called Brower's extravagance. They were also critical of his tendency to make important decisions without consulting them. Some board members were not happy about losing their tax-deductible status because of Brower's aggressive lobbying activities.

Brower's break from the Sierra Club staff finally occurred when he opposed a utility company planning to build a nuclear power plant in California's Diablo Canyon. For months, he argued about the proposed plant with the board of directors. At the time, nuclear power was thought to be a nonpolluting answer to the country's energy needs, but Brower was worried about the possible contamination from the nuclear waste that the plant would generate.

Brower and four like-minded members ran for positions on the board, intending to create a majority of board members against the Diablo Canyon site. They lost the election, and Brower was forced to resign as executive director in May 1969. While Diablo Canyon was the only significant policy disagreement between Brower and the Sierra Club during his 17 years as executive director, it was a pivotal one. "Until that moment, my other faults, which were beyond number, were tolerated, even forgiven," Brower wrote in *Let the Mountains Talk, Let the Rivers Run*. Ironically, five years later, in 1974, the club adopted a policy opposing new nuclear plant construction.

Diablo Canyon Nuclear Power Plant was constructed at a cost of nearly $6 billion. But the threat from the nearby, newly-discovered Hosgri earthquake fault has forced the plant to be decommissioned—at further cost to the public.

Despite their criticism of him, board members were aware of Brower's enormous contributions to the environmental movement—and to the Sierra Club. Under his leadership, club membership had risen from 7,000 in 1952 to 77,000 in 1969. (The group continued to grow. In 1997, the club reported a membership of 550,000.) Brower left his position knowing that the Sierra Club was no longer a hiking association for the elite but a national environmental organization with political and cultural influence. He never completely severed his ties with the Sierra Club and later became an honorary vice-president. In 1977, he received the club's highest honor, the John Muir Award. He has also received The Wilderness Society's top honor, the Robert Marshall Award, and the Thoreau Society's Medal.

In 1969, almost immediately after resigning as executive director of the Sierra Club, David Brower was named executive director of the John Muir Institute for Environmental Studies, which he cofounded in 1968. He also founded and became president of a new environmental organization, Friends of the Earth (FOE).

FOE lobbied for environmental-protection legislation and for environmentally friendly candidates. The group has been at the forefront of battles against acid rain, nuclear power, coal and oil development on public lands, as well as toxic pesticides. An early advocate of

"I've grown very fond of this planet," Brower wrote in Let the Mountains Talk, Let the Rivers Run. *"I want to help save a taste of paradise for our children."*

population control, FOE was also one of the first international environmental organizations. By 1997, Friends of the Earth was established independently in 53 countries. After nine years, Brower retired as president of FOE, but became chairman on a volunteer basis. Brower resigned from the board in 1984.

Two years earlier in 1982, David Brower had founded a third organization, Earth Island Institute, which "sponsors and develops ecological conscience in all spheres of human endeavor—a few at a time." One of the organization's most important achievements was the passage of the "dolphin safe" law. This law prohibited U.S. tuna fishers from endangering the lives of dolphins while trying to catch tuna. The institute also sponsors the Brower Fund, which provides start-up funds for new projects that take "innovative approaches to environmental problem-solving."

In the 1990s, Brower continued to serve as chairman of Earth Island Institute and speak out on environmental issues in countries all over the world. For example, at the request of the Soviet Union, he led delegations in 1988 and each year from 1990 to 1992 to Lake Baikal in Siberia to aid in its protection and restoration.

In September 1997, he said his "current delight" was that the Sierra Club directors, who did not oppose Glen Canyon Dam in 1956, now support restoring the canyon. Brower, at age 85, traveled to Washington to testify before Congress on behalf of this restoration project. He is always moving forward because, as a favorite quotation of his says, "A ship in harbor is safe, but that's not what ships are built for."

During his long environmental career, many words have been used to describe David Brower: visionary, stubborn, single-minded, charismatic, John Muir reincarnate. But never has he been called a man who played it safe.

Gaylord Anton Nelson represented the environment, as well as residents of Wisconsin, during his 18 years as a United States senator.

8

Gaylord Nelson
Senator for the Earth

*T*he future father of Earth Day was just 13 when he had his first experience as an environmental activist. Young Gaylord Nelson and his father, Anton Nelson, were traveling to a medical meeting when they passed through a town with beautiful elm trees lining its entrance. "Why can't our town have trees like that?" he asked his father.

When Gaylord returned home, he went to a town council meeting to propose planting elm trees on both sides of the road entering Clear Lake, Wisconsin. With trees touching at the top to form a beautiful arch over the road, he said, the elm trees would enhance the town's image. He even suggested a way to cut labor costs: Boy Scouts could do the planting!

As in later life, young Gaylord spoke eloquently and passionately. Unfortunately, his first endeavor in the political arena did not turn out as he had wished. The council members listened politely, but they were not persuaded. Perhaps if they had known they were being addressed by a future U.S. senator, they might have voted differently!

Gaylord Anton Nelson was born in the small town of Clear Lake in northwestern Wisconsin on June 4, 1916. His father was a doctor and once served as the town's mayor. His mother, Mary Bradt Nelson, was a nurse who also headed the Polk County Red Cross. Growing up surrounded by water, woods, and wildlife instilled in Gaylord a love of nature and a desire to protect it. He later wrote:

> There was a special adventure to being a young boy in northwestern Wisconsin. . . , exploring the deep green woods, crunching noisily through the crisp leaves on a sharp fall day, or taking a cool drink from a trout stream or a hidden lake.

Nelson graduated from San Jose State College in California in 1939 and received his law degree from the University of Wisconsin Law School in 1942. The U.S. had entered World War II the year before, so Nelson enlisted in the U.S. Army immediately following his graduation. He was stationed in Indian Town Gap, Pennsylvania, where he met Carrie Lee Dotson, a nurse. When the army shipped him to Okinawa in the South Pacific, he said good-bye to Carrie, thinking he would never see her again. How surprised and delighted he was when the army sent her to Okinawa, too! They were married in 1947 and had three children.

After leaving the army, Nelson practiced law in Madison, Wisconsin. Although he liked being a lawyer, he had always wanted to enter politics. As a young boy, his hero had been Wisconsin's U.S. Senator Robert "Fighting Bob" La Follette, who believed that the government should be an advocate for poor and working people, not just favor the rich. Young Nelson wanted to help people, too. As a child, the only thing that had worried Gaylord was that La Follette would solve all the problems before he had a chance to grow up!

Nelson's first political campaign for the Wisconsin state assembly in 1947 ended in defeat. Two years later, he tried again and won a seat in the state senate. In 1958, after serving in the state senate for 10 years, Nelson was nominated to run for governor of Wisconsin on the Democratic ticket. The campaign was difficult. The people of Wisconsin had not elected a Democratic governor since 1932. But Nelson liked people and they liked him. In addition to being intelligent and competent, he had a wonderful sense of humor and was a good storyteller. His easygoing manner won him many friends—and votes.

As governor of Wisconsin, Gaylord Nelson was determined to use his power for the good of the people and the environment. One of his proudest accomplishments was the passage of the Outdoor Recreation Acquisition Program in 1961. This program raised $50 million to buy 1 million acres of private property that were converted into public parks, wetlands, wildlife habitat, and youth camps. A one-cent tax on cigarettes funded the program, which became a model followed by other states.

In 1962, after serving four years as governor, Nelson was elected U.S. senator. On March 25, 1963, he gave his first speech in the Senate. In that speech, he asked the other 99 senators to help protect the environment:

> We cannot be blind to the growing crisis of our environment. Our soil, our water, and our air are becoming more polluted every day. Our most priceless natural resources—trees, lakes, rivers, wildlife habitats, scenic landscapes—are being destroyed.

His colleagues barely listened. In 1963, the environment was not a popular issue. Only about 20 of the 535 members of Congress called themselves environmentalists. And while these odds did not discourage Nelson, he was realistic enough to know that he could not bring the environment to the attention of the nation without help.

The man to whom Nelson turned was President John F. Kennedy. In 1963, Nelson persuaded Kennedy to take a five-day, eleven-state "resource and conservation" tour to publicize the seriously deteriorating condition of the environment. Unfortunately, the tour did not force the environment onto the agenda of national priorities.

In 1963, President John F. Kennedy and Senator Gaylord Nelson (left) embarked on a national tour to bring attention to the environment. The tour received little coverage from the media, however.

But Nelson did not give up. Characteristically, he put aside his disappointment and concentrated on passing other legislation. In 1963, Gaylord Nelson became the first member of Congress to propose banning DDT, a toxic pesticide widely used throughout the country to kill mosquitoes and other insects.

DDT was dangerous because, once sprayed, it remained in the environment—in bodies of water, in soil, in trees and plants—and contaminated the food chain. For example, if DDT was sprayed near a lake, it would leach into the lake and be absorbed by the lake's *plankton*, the tiny plant and animal organisms in the water. Fish in the lake would then eat the plankton, and raptors, birds of prey such as bald eagles and peregrine falcons, would eat the fish. These birds would then lay eggs with shells too weak to hold their chicks. Scientists blamed DDT for the decline in the raptor populations.

The efforts of Nelson and scientist Rachel Carson, author of *Silent Spring* (a 1962 book that detailed the problems of pesticide use), to secure a ban on DDT met strong opposition from the chemical companies that produced the pesticide. But the perseverance of Nelson, Carson, and others paid off when, nine years later, in 1972, the Environmental Protection Agency finally banned the use of DDT.

Senator Nelson also cosponsored the landmark 1964 Wilderness Act. This congressional act created the National Wilderness Preservation System and protected as wilderness more than 9 million acres of national forest, park, and wildlife refuges. In 1980, he cosponsored the Alaska Lands Act, which added 56 million acres to the Wilderness System. Today, more than 104 million acres of America's wildlands are protected as wilderness.

What is remarkable about Senator Gaylord Nelson's environmental record in Congress is not only that he sponsored or cosponsored so many major environmental

The first views of Earth from space dramatically widened people's perspectives about their home planet, giving them a new appreciation of its beauty and fragility. This photograph was taken by Apollo 11 astronauts on their way to the moon in July 1969.

137

laws, but that he was also often the first to do so. He was the first to introduce legislation mandating increased fuel-efficiency standards for automobiles. Senator Nelson also presented the first bill requiring the restoration of land that had been scarred by strip mining. Again, the opposition of commercial interests—this time, mining companies—played a role in delaying passage of strip-mining legislation. But in 1977 Congress passed the Surface Mining Control and Reclamation Act, a bill very similar to the one proposed by Nelson many years earlier.

Nelson was also the first member of Congress to call for a ban on the use of Agent Orange. The U.S. Army had used this highly toxic herbicide during the Vietnam War to defoliate trees that hid enemy soldiers. Agent Orange has since been blamed for the health problems of many Vietnam War veterans and Vietnamese civilians. In the United States, the government killed trees with Agent Orange so that farmers could use the cleared areas as pasture. When Nelson proposed a ban on Agent Orange in 1968, only a handful of his colleagues voted with him. Despite overwhelming opposition to his bill, Nelson continued his battle against the dangerous herbicide. Fifteen years later, in 1983, Congress finally passed legislation prohibiting the use of Agent Orange.

The Appalachian Trail, the best-known and most widely used hiking trail in the United States, extends for 2,100 miles from Maine to Georgia. It crosses public lands, such as national forests, as well as private lands

This section of the Appalachian Trail in Maryland is part of the nationwide trail system that Gaylord Nelson proposed to Congress.

with the consent of the owners. In the 1960s, many parts of the trail were being closed by private landowners.

Senator Gaylord Nelson knew that the only way to save the magnificent trail was by congressional action. Between 1964 and 1968, he introduced several proposals that would authorize the purchase of the necessary private lands. On October 2, 1968, President Lyndon Johnson signed into law Nelson's proposal to save the Appalachian Trail and to create a nationwide system of hiking trails.

139

Although the Kennedy tour of 1963 had failed to bring the environment to the attention of the public, Nelson continued to look for some major event to wake up citizens and Congress and force them to pay attention to the condition of the environment. One day in 1969, Nelson read an article about a new antiwar tactic. At that time, many college students and faculty protested the war in Vietnam by holding *teach-ins*—seminars, classes, and other activities—to educate citizens about the war. The teach-ins were a huge success. Suddenly, Nelson had an idea. Why not sponsor a nationwide teach-in about the environment? Perhaps this was the major event he had been seeking.

As soon as he got back to Washington, D.C., Nelson began raising money to fund the event, later called "Earth Day." He wrote letters to the governors of all 50 states and to the mayors of major cities, suggesting a nationwide demonstration of concern for the environment. Believing that the youth of America were important to the country's future, Nelson wrote an article about Earth Day and sent it to all the college newspapers in the country as well as to *Scholastic Magazine*, which was received by most grade schools and high schools.

In September 1969, during a speech in Seattle, Washington, Nelson announced that in the spring of 1970 there would be a national environmental teach-in. This time the press paid attention and gave the upcoming Earth Day celebration a good deal of coverage.

140

"Earth Day Every Day" became a popular slogan to remind people that their environment needs constant care.

About 20 million people participated in demonstrations across the country on April 22, 1970, the first Earth Day. At least 10,000 grade schools and high schools, 2,000 colleges, and 1,000 communities were involved in some sort of Earth Day activity. Among Earth Day "happenings" were the following:

• Congress adjourned for the day so that members of the House and the Senate could attend and speak at environmental events in their districts. Some members of Congress used Nelson's environmental speeches as models for their own remarks.

• The Reynolds Metals Company sent trucks to pick up aluminum cans collected at "trash-ins" at colleges in 14 states.

• Schoolchildren pulled soda pop bottles and other trash out of rivers.

• In New York City, Mayor John Lindsey closed Fifth Avenue to automobile traffic for an Earth Day parade, and more than 100,000 people attended an ecology fair in Central Park.

• In Centralia, Washington, a goat wandered around a lawn wearing a sign reading: "I eat garbage, what are you doing for your community?"

Earth Day turned out to be everything that Senator Nelson hoped it would be. *American Heritage* magazine called Earth Day "one of the most remarkable happenings in the history of democracy." Nelson was quick to point out that its success depended on the grassroots efforts of ordinary people and communities. "If you want to move the nation to make hard decisions on important issues," he said, "the grassroots is the source of power. With it you can do anything, without it nothing."

Earth Day inspired a burst of legislative activity in Congress and in all 50 states. During the following decade, Congress passed 28 major pieces of environmental legislation, including the Clean Air Act of 1970 to

142

reduce air pollution; the Federal Water Pollution Control Act Amendments of 1972, which curtailed pollutants being dumped into rivers and lakes; the Endangered Species Act, which protects the habitat of animals whose living space might be threatened; and additions to the wilderness system.

By 1980, Gaylord Nelson was one of the most respected members of Congress. A *Washingtonian* magazine article rating the best and worst members of Congress, called Nelson the "most-liked" senator. That popularity is why his loss in the election of 1980 came as such a shock. Unhappy with the way President Jimmy Carter, a Democrat, had been leading the country, the American people elected Ronald Reagan, a Republican, as president. Many members of Congress, including Senator Nelson, were also defeated simply because they, like Carter, were Democrats.

Gaylord Nelson was not bitter about his defeat, however. Instead, he saw it as an opportunity to carry on his work in a different way. As counsel to The Wilderness Society—a nonprofit environmental organization working to protect America's public lands and its remaining wilderness areas—Gaylord Nelson works on behalf of the environment with the same enthusiasm and dedication he had as a 13-year-old boy asking the town council of Clear Lake, Wisconsin, to plant elm trees.

Each year on April 22, Earth Day is observed in the United States. It is both a celebration and a reminder that

Americans continue to show their concern about the environment, as demonstrated by this well-attended observance of Earth Day 1990 on the Mall in Washington, D.C.

144

the state of the environment is vitally important to the quality of each person's life and to the lives of the generations that will follow.

On September 29, 1995, President Bill Clinton awarded the Presidential Medal of Freedom to Gaylord Nelson. In presenting the medal, the president said:

> Twenty-five years ago this year, Americans came together for the very first Earth Day. . . . And they came together, more than anything else, because of one American—Gaylord Nelson. . . . As the father of Earth Day, he is the grandfather of all that grew out of that event—the Environmental Protection Act, the Clean Air Act, the Clean Water Act, the Safe Drinking Water Act. I hope that Gaylord Nelson's shining example will illuminate all the debates in this city for years to come.

Two spectacular sights in Yosemite National Park: El Capitan on the left and Bridalveil Falls on the right

146

America's Public Lands

The **National Park System** is administered by the **National Park Service**, established by Congress in 1916. The park service is a bureau of the U.S. Department of the Interior and oversees approximately 83 million acres of land set aside for conservation or cultural purposes.

The park service's responsibility includes the 51 areas of the United States that have been preserved as **national parks** for all citizens to visit and enjoy because of their natural beauty or other outstanding features.

The National Park Service is also in charge of national memorials, national lakeshores and seashores, national wild and scenic rivers, national historic sites, including battlefields, and national trails, such as the Appalachian and Lewis and Clark Trails.

In 1891, Congress authorized the president to create **forest reserves** to protect timberland from unregulated use. The reserves were designated **national forests** in 1907. The **National Forest System** is administered by the **National Forest Service** of the U.S. Department of Agriculture. The system includes all national forests and national grasslands. Lumbering, mining, grazing, and recreation are permitted within limits in national forests.

National Wildlife Refuges ensure the survival of wildlife by creating areas for wildlife to breed, rest, and feed. Some limited hunting and recreation activities are permitted. The **Fish and Wildlife Service**, part of the Department of the Interior, oversees refuges.

The **National Wilderness Preservation System** was created by the U.S. Wilderness Act of 1964. The legislation set aside 9 million acres in 54 areas to be preserved in their natural condition—wild and undeveloped. Because the act also provided for designation of future wilderness areas, the system now includes approximately 104 million acres. Many of these wilderness areas are located within national parks or forests.

Sources of Information

The following government agencies and environmental organizations, many of which are mentioned in this book, will help you learn more about the history of conservation and current environmental issues.

GOVERNMENT AGENCIES

Environmental Protection
  Agency
401 M Street, SW
Washington, D.C. 20460
202-260-2090
Internet: http://www.epa.gov

National Forest Service
U.S. Dept. of Agriculture
PO Box 96090
Washington, D.C. 20090-6090
202-205-1760

National Oceanic and
  Atmospheric Administration
14th & Constitution Ave., NW
Washington, D.C. 20230
202-482-6090

National Park Service
U.S. Dept. of the Interior
1849 C Street, NW
Washington, D.C. 20240
Information: 202-208-4747

Natural Resources
  Conservation Service
U.S. Dept. of Agriculture
14th & Independence Ave., SW
Washington, D.C. 20250
202-720-3210

U.S. Department of Agriculture
14th & Independence Ave., SW
Washington, D.C. 20250
Information: 202-720-2791
Internet: http://www.usda.gov

U.S. Department of Energy
Forrestal Building
1000 Independence Ave., SW
Washington, D.C. 20585
Internet: http://www.doe.gov

U. S. Department of the
  Interior
1849 C Street, NW
Washington, D.C. 20240
Information: 202-208-3100
Internet:
  http://www.usgs.gov.doi

ENVIRONMENTAL ORGANIZATIONS

Appalachian Trail Conference
PO Box 807
Harpers Ferry, WV 25425
304-535-6331
Internet: www.atconf.org

Rachel Carson Council, Inc.
8940 Jones Mill Road
Chevy Chase, MD 20815
301-652-1877
Internet: http://members.aol.
com/rcccouncil/ourpage/rcc_
page.htm

J. N. "Ding" Darling
Foundation
881 Ocean Drive, #17E
Key Biscayne, FL 33149
305-361-9788

Defenders of Wildlife
Suite 1400
1101 14th Street, NW
Washington, D.C. 20005
202-682-9400
Internet:
http://www.defenders.org

Earth Island Institute
Suite 28
300 Broadway
San Francisco, CA 94133
415-788-3666

Environmental Defense Fund
257 Park Avenue South
New York, NY 10010
212-505-2100
Internet: www.edf.org

Friends of the Earth
The Global Building
Suite 300
1025 Vermont Avenue, NW
Washington, D.C. 20005
202-783-7400
Internet: http://www.foe.org

Hawk Mountain Sanctuary
Association
1700 Hawk Mountain Road
Kempton, PA 19529-9449
610-756-6961
Internet:
www.hawkmountain.org

Kids for Saving Earth Worldwide
5425 Pineview Lane
Plymouth, MN 55442
612-559-0602
E-mail: kseww@aol.com

National Arbor Day
Foundation
100 Arbor Avenue
Nebraska City, NE 68410
402-474-5655
Internet:
http://www.arborday.org

National Audubon Society
700 Broadway
New York, NY 10003-9562
212-979-3000

National Parks and
  Conservation Association
1776 Massachusetts Ave., NW
Washington, D.C. 20036-1904
202-223-6722
E-mail: natparks@aol.com

National Wildlife Federation
8925 Leesburg Pike
Vienna, VA 22184-0001
703-790-4000
Internet: http://www.nwf.org

The Nature Conservancy
1815 North Lynn Street
Arlington, VA 22209
703-841-5300
Internet: http://www.tnc.org

The Sierra Club
85 Second Street
San Francisco, CA 94105-3441
415-977-5653 or 5566
Internet: http://www.sierra-
  club.org

U.S. PIRG
218 D Street, SE
Washington, D.C. 20003
202-546-9707
Internet: pirg@pirg.org
  http://www.pirg.org/uspirg

The Wilderness Society
900 17th Street, NW
Washington, D.C. 20006-2596
202-833-2300

World Wildlife Fund
Suite 500
1250 24th Street, NW
Washington, D.C. 20037
202-293-4800
Internet:
  www.worldwildlife.org

*Olaus Murie
often painted
the animals he
studied.*

150

Bibliography

Axelrod, Alan, and Charles Phillips. *The Environmentalists: A Biographical Dictionary from the 17th Century to the Present*. New York: Facts on File, 1993.

Brooks, Paul. *The House of Life: Rachel Carson at Work*. Boston: Houghton Mifflin, 1972.

Broun, Maurice. *Hawks Aloft: The Story of Hawk Mountain*. New York: Dodd, Mead, 1984.

Brower, David Ross. *Let the Mountains Talk, Let the Rivers Run*. San Francisco: Harper Collins, 1995.

Carson, Rachel. *Silent Spring*. Boston: Houghton Mifflin, 1962.

Clarke, James Mitchell. *The Life and Adventures of John Muir*. San Francisco: Sierra Club, 1979.

Davis, Richard C., ed. *Encyclopedia of American Forest and Conservation History*, vols. 1 and 2. New York: Macmillan, 1983.

Flader, Susan L. *Thinking Like a Mountain: Aldo Leopold and the Evolution of an Ecological Attitude toward Deer, Wolves and Forests*. Columbia: University of Missouri Press, 1974.

Fox, Stephen R. *John Muir and His Legacy: The American Conservation Movement*. Boston: Little, Brown, 1981.

Graham, Frank, Jr., and Carl W. Buchheister. *The Audubon Ark: A History of the National Audubon Society*. New York: Knopf, 1990.

Graham, Frank, Jr. *Man's Dominion: The Story of Conservation in America*. New York: M. Evans, 1971.

Grossman, Mark. *The ABC-CLIO Companion to the Environmental Movement*. Santa Barbara: ABC-CLIO, 1994.

Harwood, Michael. *The View from Hawk Mountain*. New York: Scribner's, 1973.

Hoyle, Russ. *Gale Environmental Almanac.* Detroit: Gale, 1993.

Keene, Ann T. *Earthkeepers: Observers and Protectors of Nature.* New York: Oxford University Press, 1994.

Lear, Linda. *Rachel Carson: Witness for Nature.* New York: Holt, 1997.

Lendt, David L. *Ding: The Life of Jay Norwood Darling.* Ames: Iowa State University Press, 1979.

Lorbiecki, Marybeth. *Aldo Leopold: A Fierce Green Fire.* Helena, Mont.: Falcon, 1996.

Meine, Curt. *Aldo Leopold: His Life and Work.* Madison: University of Wisconsin Press, 1988.

Murie, Olaus J. *The Elk of North America.* Harrisburg, Penn.: Stackpole, 1951.

——— *Journeys to the Far North.* Palo Alto, Calif.: American West, 1973.

Scheffer, Victor B. *The Shaping of Environmentalism in America.* Seattle: University of Washington Press, 1991.

Snow, Donald, ed. *Voices from the Environmental Movement: Perspectives for a New Era.* Washington, D.C.: Island Press, 1992.

Stroud, Richard H., ed. *National Leaders of American Conservation.* Washington, D.C.: Smithsonian Institution Press, 1985.

Turner, Frederick. *Rediscovering America: John Muir in His Time and Ours.* New York: Viking, 1985.

Vickery, Jim Dale. *Wilderness Visionaries.* Minocqua, Wisc.: North Word Press, 1986, 1994.

Whitman, Sylvia. *This Land is Your Land: The American Conservation Movement.* Minneapolis: Lerner, 1994.

Wild, Peter. *Pioneer Conservationists of Western America.* Missoula, Mont.: Mountain Press, 1979.

Index

Green River, 118
Grinnell, George Bird, 58
gun manufacturers, 10, 46, 51,
    56, 58, 60, 63, 76

Hall, Harry C., 73
Harrison, Benjamin, 32
Hawk Mountain Sanctuary, 67,
    110; Association, 64
herbicides, 98, 138
Hetch Hetchy Valley, 35, 36,
    37, 118, 119-120
Hines, Robert W., 102
Hornaday, William, 60, 61
Howe, Quincy, 101
Huckins, Olga Owens, 104
hunting, 7-8, 10, 51, 52, 60, 63,
    64, 72, 73, 87; of ducks, 41,
    42, 44, 46
Hutchings, James, 26, 28

Ickes, Harold, 66
Ingersoll, Mrs. Raymond V., 65
insects, 16, 97, 98, 103-104,
    106, 136
Interior, Department of, 111,
    118
Internal Revenue Service, 123
Inuits, 85
Island Between, 94

Jackson, William Henry, 13
James, Henry, 31
J. N. "Ding" Darling
    Foundation, 52
J. N. "Ding" Darling National
    Wildlife Refuge, 53
John Muir Award, 94, 127
John Muir Institute for
    Environmental Studies, 127
Johns Hopkins University, 100
Johnson, Lyndon, 18, 93, 139
Johnson, Robert Underwood,

30, 31-32
Journey to the Far North, 84

Kennedy, John F., 109, 134-
    135, 140
Key Deer Refuge Bill, 52
Kings Canyon National Park,
    66, 124

Lacey Antiquities Act, 35
La Follette, Robert "Fighting
    Bob," 133
Land and Water Conservation
    Fund Act of 1964, 125
Le Conte, Joseph, 36
Leonard, Dick, 115
Leopold, Aldo, 10; arboretum
    established by, 79; death of,
    81; early years of, 71;
    education of, 71; as forester,
    14, 44, 69, 70, 71-72, 73, 74,
    76; and founding Wilderness
    Society, 15-16, 79; interest
    of, in game management, 74,
    76, 78; philosophy of, 68, 69,
    70, 74, 81; as professor at
    University of Wisconsin, 44,
    78-79; writings of, 69, 70, 72,
    74, 75, 76, 78, 79, 80-81
Leopold, Carl (father), 71
Leopold, Clara Starker
    (mother), 71
Leopold, Estella (daughter), 81
Leopold, Estella Bergere (wife),
    72, 74, 80, 81
Leopold, Nina (daughter), 80
*Let the Mountains Talk, Let the
    Rivers Run*, 121, 126, 128
Lewis and Clark Trail, 52-53
Life, 125
Lindsey, John, 142
logging, 9, 15, 26, 30, 33, 64, 74

ABOUT THE AUTHOR

PATRICIA BYRNES, a book editor, was previously managing editor of *Wilderness*, the quarterly magazine of The Wilderness Society, for which she wrote numerous articles on wilderness and environmental issues. She co-edited, with T. H. Watkins, *The World of Wilderness: Essays on the Power and Purpose of Wild Country* (Reinhart, 1995) and has written articles for several publications, including the *Washington Post*. A graduate of George Washington University, Byrnes lives in Baltimore.

Photo Credits

Photographs courtesy of: cover (front), pp. 8, 10, 12, 13, 31, 61, Library of Congress; cover (background), 43, 58 (left, Tom Smylie), 70 (Dave Mech), 86 (John Sarvis), 102 (Rex Gary Schmidt), 124 (Fran Mauer), U. S. Fish and Wildlife Services; p. 6, Minnesota Historical Society; pp. 15, 18, 20, 34, 77, 78, 82, 88, 92, 95, 112, 130, 135, 141, 144, 150, The Wilderness Society; pp. 17, 122, National Archives; pp. 19, 105, Archive Photos; pp. 24 (WHiX340814), 28 (WHiX35766), The State Historical Society of Wisconsin; pp. 27, 29, 146, Yosemite National Park Research Library; p. 36 (both), Colby Memorial Library, Sierra Club; pp. 38, 47, 48, 50, 53, Jay Norwood "Ding" Darling Foundation; p. 45 (left), Franklin D. Roosevelt Library; p. 45 (right), State Historical Society of Iowa; pp. 54, 65, Hawk Mountain Sanctuary; p. 58 (right), *Famous 19th Century Faces*, Art Direct Book Co.; p. 59, American Museum of Natural History; pp. 68, 73, 80, University of Wisconsin—Madison Archives; pp. 96 (Brooks Photographers), 99, 110 (Shirley A. Briggs), Rachel Carson History Project; pp. 116, 120, 128, Earth Island Institute; p. 137, NASA; p. 139, University of Maryland Libraries, *Baltimore News American* Collection.